AN AMERICAN CHILD'S PORTFOLIO

THE ART OF
SAVING & INVESTING
FOR CHILDREN

DR. DENNIS PAULAHA

Patron Books

Distributed by:
Burgess International Group, Inc.
7110 Ohms Lane
Edina, Minnesota 55439
Phone: (612) 831-1344, Fax: (612) 831-3167

Patron Books

To my wife Deborah
and my children,
Katharine and Sarah

Contents

A Note to the Reader

When asked why they climb mountains, some mountain climbers answer, "Because they are there."

Others say, "If you have to ask, you probably won't understand."

Both responses apply to this book.

There are mountains I hope we can help our children climb--just because they are there.

And if you have to ask why we should help our children climb those mountains, this book is probably not for you. This book is for everyone who does not have to ask the question.

--Dennis Paulaha

Introduction

Button your shirt from the bottom up.

This is a book about how to save and invest for your children.

It is based on a simple principle that my father taught me when I was very young--a principle I have used every day of my life since then.

It was to button my shirt from the bottom up.

I believe that this "philosophy" applies to just about everything in life.

By starting at the bottom--getting the bottom straight before you begin--you can get almost anything right the first time.

You will almost never have to back-track and start over.

And by the time you get to the more difficult stuff-- the buttons at the top that are not so easy to see--it will be almost impossible to make a mistake.

If you know you can get it right the first time, you will not waste your time and energy thinking about things that will take care of themselves.

Some of the ideas in this book were developed while I was researching and writing about economic and financial issues for the public. But the advice is practical and personal. It is, in large part, a retelling of what I learned while determining what I could and could not do for my own young children: Katharine (born in December 1984) and Sarah (born in September 1987).

You Can Begin Today

The First Step

In this first section, you will see how to get started on a financial plan that can add thousands of dollars to your child's future.

You will not have to leave the house. You will not have to call an outside expert. And you can do it with money you might not think you have.

The Shoe-box Portfolio

Begin with a shoe box.
Get a shoe box. And start filling it with money.
What money?
The money that friends and relatives give to your child.

There is no better first step you can make in preparing a solid financial plan for your children.

Whether you are an expectant parent, a new parent, or the parent of a four, five, or ten year old, you can use a shoe box. But the sooner you begin, the better.

If you get started before your child is born, you will have a place to collect baby-shower money.

But no matter when you get started, whenever your child receives gift money, put it in the box.

And whenever you can, throw in some of your spare change.

Instead of spending your child's gift money on cute little things, you will be saving it.

It might not seem like a lot of money at first. But it is worth much more than you might think.

Best of all, you will have set up a real financial plan.

And once you have established your "shoe-box financial program," the "bigger" saving and investing decisions that come later will seem easy. They will simply be additions to what you already have.

Remember getting money when you were a child? A small amount of money, by adult standards, was a big deal.

We all had a favorite aunt, uncle, or grandparent who slipped us a dollar at family gatherings, or who sent us five or ten dollars on our birthdays.

Whatever it was, it always seemed like a lot of money, especially to a five or six year old.

What is the difference between "kid money" and "adult money?"

Partly, it has to do with what we buy. Kids can buy very important things for less than a dollar. The things adults think are important seem to cost hundreds or thousands of dollars.

So it is easy to lose track of all the five- or ten-dollar gifts our children receive. And it is difficult for adults think about using such money to create a real "portfolio."

But if you put birthday, holiday, and family-gathering money into your shoe box, before you know it, you will have easily saved $100 to $200, maybe much more.

The next step is to turn the "kid money" into "adult money."

Saving a child's gift-money in a shoe box is pure common sense.

Deciding what to do with the money as it accumulates has to make financial sense.

I have three favorite investments for small amounts of money. One is to open an account that pays money-market interest rates (short-term rates). The second is to buy zero-coupon Treasury bonds. The third, especially if you meet the restrictions that we will look at later, is to buy Series EE savings bonds.

If you put $250 in a money market account that pays eight percent interest, year after year, the $250 will double in nine years and double again in the next nine years. In eighteen years it will be worth $1,000.

If you buy a zero-coupon Treasury bond for about $200 to $250 for your one-year old, it will be worth $1,000 before he or she is out of college.

If you buy $250 worth of Series EE savings bonds and hold them for about 20 years, they too will be worth $1,000.

You can buy Series EE bonds for as little as $25 each. The interest is always free of state and local taxes. And if you meet the income restrictions, and use the money for education, *the interest is totally tax free!*

Therefore, every two- to three-hundred dollars you save and invest while your child is young can be worth a future one-thousand dollars.

Put another way, you can easily let thousands of dollars in future money slip through your fingers if you do not have a simple way to save small amounts of cash.

That is why the shoe box is so important.

It will help you secure thousands of dollars for your child's future.

It will also let you see how easy it is to put a financial plan into action.

Later, I will explain why interest-bearing accounts, zero-coupon bonds, and Series EE savings bonds are my favorite choices for a child's portfolio. I will also examine a number of other opportunities. You may agree with my choices. Or you may like some of the others better.

But whatever you choose, it should be measured against these three choices.

But is putting money in a shoe box a *real* financial plan?

It certainly is. It is as real as anything an expensive consultant can dream up.

Of course, it is a limited plan.

Although it can provide thousands of dollars for your child's future, you will probably want to do more.

But doing more can be, and should be, just as simple and easy.

Without an easy way to collect "small change," I can guarantee you that you will lose thousands of future dollars your children could have had.

And without an easy way to deal with more "sophisticated" investments, I can virtually guarantee you that bigger opportunities will disappear as well.

You might be thinking that I am using a shoe box as an analogy, as a way to make a point about financial planning. I can promise you, I am not. I am absolutely serious when I tell you to get something you can use to collect small amounts of money.

Let me tell you why.

One of the major obstacles to saving and investing for our children is that the best time to make investments for children is when they are very young. Unfortunately, that is also the time when most of us can least afford to put much money into our children's accounts.

The older we get, and the older our children get, the better we can afford to make investments for our children.

But the fact of life about investments is that they grow over time!

The more time they have to earn interest or appreciate in value, the more they will be worth.

As a result, your "shoe-box portfolio" can be the equal of thousands of dollars transferred to children when they are in their teens.

So there is a practical reason for doing as much as you can when your children are very young.

And one thing we can all do is to make certain that the money our young children receive does not slip away.

Besides, there are only three significant differences between our simple beginning and a more "sophisticated" plan:

1) As your plans become bigger, you will need a "bigger shoe box"--some sort of child's account.

2) As your portfolio grows, you may want to consider other investment possibilities.

3) The more money that is involved, the more you will want to consider the tax consequences of your actions.

But the principles remain the same:

Save money in an easy-to-deal-with place.

As the money accumulates, transfer it to an account where it will earn interest or use it to purchase other assets.

In what follows, we will see what is necessary to prepare bigger plans.

But if you get a shoe box, you will have made the right start. You will be buttoning your shirt from the bottom up.

Summary

Although we have not yet discussed the details of our three basic investments, this first chapter is a complete, stand-alone financial program.

If you do nothing more than what we have already discussed, you will have a successful financial plan for your child:

- Get a shoe box to save the gift-money your child receives.
- Add some of your loose change whenever you can.
- Periodically transfer the cash to an interest-bearing account.
- Use some of the money to purchase zero-coupon Treasury bonds.
- Use some of the money to buy Series EE savings bonds. (In order to qualify for the tax free interest, your income has to be less than $60,000 in the year the bonds are cashed, and the money has to be used for education--your child's, yours, or your spouse's. I will discuss Series EE savings bonds again later.)

I hope you will read on. I hope you want to do more. But if you limit your plans to what has already been discussed, your children will already be assured of a better start in life.

Three Principles of Success

Before we go on, I want to discuss three important investment principles:

1) Keep it simple.
2) Relax.
3) Take control.

Using our shirt-buttoning analogy one more time, these three principles represent buttoning the next three buttons.

Although these principles may seem obvious, they are easy to forget. And if you forget the basics, your plans can go astray before you know what happened.

Many people believe that financial plans are cut-and-dried, follow-the-rules kinds of activities. They are not. Financial plans are as much a way of thinking as a way of acting. If that were not true, everyone would be equally successful, which is not the case.

To be successful, you have to follow the basic principles of success.

Keep it simple

A few years ago, one of the most talked about inventions was the video-phone--the telephone with a built in television that let you see who you were talking to.

The video-phone sounded like one of the greatest inventions since the wheel. And not long ago a small number of fully-working models were manufactured and installed.

Dr. Robert Lucky, director of research for AT&T's Bell Labs, owned one of those first models. But when Dr. Lucky was interviewed by Bill Moyers on public television, he explained how, one-by-one, the other owners sent their phones back.

Eventually, Robert Lucky owned the last working video-phone in the world.

What happened? Why did the video-phone fail? Why did those who owned them send them back? Why did everyone else fail to rush down to their local phone distribution center and demand to be next in line to have this great miracle installed in their homes?

Because the video-phone was a bad idea!

It was a good idea--as an idea. But in practice--in actual, honest-to-goodness use--the video-phone was a terrible product.

As Dr. Lucky explained, it was too demanding.

It was sometimes fun to see the person you were talking to.

It was not much fun being seen.

If you have to stare into a camera while you are talking, you cannot do anything else. The video-phone demands your entire presence. It demands your entire thought process.

If someone asked you to prepare an advertisement for a video-phone, what would you write?

"Get the phone that lets you see who you're talking to!"

Or:

"Get the phone that lets everyone who calls watch your every move!"

A video-phone can be fun. It can also be a real intrusion into your private life.

The plain old telephone is a marvel. It does exactly what we want it to do. It lets us communicate easily with others. It is simple. It is easy to use. You can do other things while you are talking. It gets the job done.

But if you make the product *better, more advanced,* you can destroy some of its benefits.

Financial plans are the same. Some are simple and basic and get the job done. Others demand more than they give.

The basic purpose of saving and investing for our children is to give them a better chance for a successful and happy life.

Keep it simple, it works. Complicate it--devise a plan that is too demanding--it is doomed. It will end up sharing shelf-space with all the old video-phones.

And the children lose.

Much of what is written about saving and investing, either for adults or children, sounds exciting. It sounds fantastically easy and profitable. It can sound like the greatest idea since the wheel.

In practice, the pie-in-the-sky benefits are often overshadowed by extra costs, extra demands on your time and energy, and greater risks.

You do not need a financial plan for your children that is the equivalent of a video-phone or even a car phone. You need a plan you can implement and follow, not a plan that follows you around wherever you go, ringing in your ears.

What most of us need is a basic financial plan, something like a basic telephone service.

If you have such a plan, you are almost assured of making your life and the lives of your children better.

Relax

A few years ago, a financial writer published a book of ideas for financing a college education.

One of the ideas was to purchase a rental-house near the college your child attends. Instead of paying for a dormitory or apartment, your child lives in the house. To help pay for the mortgage, your child rents out rooms to other students. And when your son or daughter graduates, the house is sold for a profit that recovers a large part of his or her tuition and book expenses.

Sounds good. I am sure the plan could work. It probably has worked. But if you are not already a real-estate investor, you may not want to manage property half-way across the country.

Besides, if your children are going to be landlords and maintenance people while they are in college:

What will happen to their grades?

What will happen during vacations?

Who will be responsible for the property during the summer?

Plus--real estate profits are far from guaranteed, especially if you are going to hold the property for only four years. Rents might not cover the mortgage. And any house can lose value.

In the end, you could end up with real-estate losses on top of college costs, while also disrupting your children's lives and grades.

Such schemes can also stab your other plans in the back. By assuming that you have college expenses all "figured out," you may decide it is OK to drop your real financial plans. In effect, you could end up betting your child's future on a financial scheme you may not be able to put into practice when the time comes.

The "buy-a-rental-house" college-financing scheme is simply a real estate investment plan. If you believe that real estate is a good investment, do it yourself-- now. Don't wait until your children are in college to buy a house for them to manage. Buy one now and manage it yourself, with the idea that the profits will be used to finance a future college education.

But don't mix everything together.

More importantly: relax. Stick with simple ideas that make sense to you. Have fun with what you are doing.

Over the years, you will run into hundreds of invest-ment schemes for your children.

Each time, ask yourself the following four questions:

1) "Will it take time I don't have?"

2) "Is it something I can actually do?"

3) "Is there a risk of losing all or part of my invest-ment—including the time it demands?"

4) "Will it take funds away from my basic investment plan?"

Most of the ideas you will read about are specialized plans for people with special skills, knowledge, and circumstances. Few have anything to offer the average family.

It would be nice if we could all take advantage of every clever idea. But that will not happen.

So instead of dreaming about the video-phones we cannot have, it is better to think about what we can do.

If you relax and stick to a plan that fits your own family's circumstances and needs, you will be more successful and happier.

Take control

A friend of mine--also an economist--thought it might be fun, and profitable, to be a stock broker for a while. After teaching for ten years, he wanted a break from the academic life. He thought he knew a lot about what stock brokers are supposed to know. He also thought he knew something about dealing with people. After all, students are people.

He saw an ad from a national brokerage company in the local paper. They were looking for stock brokers. So he called.

He expected them to be impressed by his Ph.D. and all his years of teaching experience. He was certain he would be a successful broker. He was certain he was one of the most qualified candidates ever to respond to one of their ads.

What more could they possibly want?

They wanted a good vacuum-cleaner salesman.

That's what the sales manager told him.

The sales manager was so certain that my friend's economic training would be a detriment rather than an asset that my friend could not even get an interview.

Why a vacuum-cleaner salesman instead of a trained economist?

Because a stock broker is primarily a salesperson. His or her job is to sell you investments that will, hopefully, meet your "needs."

The fact is, we buy most of our investments from salespeople.

If you want straightforward, personal investment advice and counseling, you are going to have to pay for it.

But if you are like most of us, you are going to get a lot of "advice" and "counseling" from people who earn their livings by selling you something.

There is nothing wrong with salespeople. They help us buy what we want, from our homes, cars, clothing, computers, vacuum cleaners, and television sets to our investments in stocks, bonds, real estate, precious metals, and fine art.

The best salespeople take their jobs very seriously.

In fact, a good salesperson can be more knowledgeable than a not-so-dedicated consultant. Some of the most successful salespeople actually *sell knowledge*. They do the work we do not have time for and give us legitimate choices to make--choices that can help us meet our own individual objectives.

But--and this is what is important--you can run into big trouble if you forget that salespeople are salespeople and assume that they can do more than they can do.

I do not want to imply that salespeople cannot be trusted. That is not true. But I do want to state as clearly as possible that they should not be trusted to provide advice and knowledge they cannot be expected to have. Especially when that advice is crucial to our children's future.

As a rule, the salespeople you work with have your best interests in mind. They earn a living by selling investments to steady clients. And to keep steady clients happy, salespeople have to try their best.

The point of the vacuum-cleaner salesman story is not to make you overly suspicious of brokers. It is to help you see that you must accept the responsibility of guiding your own plan.

Many, maybe most, of your investments will be purchased through stock brokers.

If you are clear about your objectives and about the risk you are willing to accept (I normally prefer "no risk"), you can get a lot of help from brokers. They have access to more information and investment products than you will ever need.

But you should not hand control over to your broker. Not because your broker cannot be trusted, but because your broker cannot be expected to have either the training or the time to be your own personal financial planner and manager.

That is your job.

Summary of a basic financial plan.

As simple as it might sound, if you follow the advice in our first two chapters, you will have a real financial plan in place.

· You will have decided to save money for your child.

· You will have an easy and accessible place to save the money--a shoe box, paper bag, or whatever.

· You will have something to do with the money as it accumulates:

Put it in an interest-bearing account at a brokerage firm or bank.

Purchase zero-coupon U.S. Treasury bonds from your stock broker.

Buy Series EE savings bonds from your bank or savings institution.

Or invest in some other assets.

· You will have decided to keep it simple--to concentrate on a straightforward plan. No "video-phone" financial programs.

· You will have decided to relax--to not to let all sorts of investment schemes sidetrack your simple, basic plan.

· You will have recognized that you--not a salesperson--must be the ultimate manager, that you must be in control.

· You will have guaranteed your children a better financial future.

· You will have accomplished more than the vast majority of Americans.

One final note: If you are relatively wealthy, you may be thinking that a shoe-box investment plan is not for you. That may be true.

But I want you to think about an important fact. The wealthier you are, the more "loose money" is going to come your child's way. Your child will probably receive more and larger cash gifts than other children. Therefore, the future value of the money you are likely to spend without thinking will be considerably greater as well.

In a few minutes, we will look more closely at our three basic investments: insured interest-bearing accounts, zero-coupon Treasury bonds, and Series EE savings bonds.

We will also examine a number of alternative investment opportunities.

For now, it is enough to know that at least three simple, "no-risk," perfectly legitimate investment choices exist. And that each can be purchased for a small amount of money--as little as $25!

But before examining your investment options, I want to talk about need.

And about how to give money to children.

Need

We all have goals or objectives.

And we all make assumptions about what is needed to reach those goals.

One of our most important goals is to help our children have the best life possible.

But what assumptions are we making about our children's future?

And how accurate or realistic are they?

Here is a list of seven common assumptions.

ASSUMPTION 1:

"Each generation of Americans does better than the last."

That used to be true.

But, little by little, the "good old days" are whatever is past. If you are part of the generation with young children today, chances are you may not be doing as well as your parents' generation.

And the odds are it will be even more difficult for your children to afford marriage, kids, homes, and peace-of-mind.

ASSUMPTION 2:
"Education is the great equalizer. The way to get ahead is to get an education."

That is true. But with a huge qualifier: It may make a big difference where your children get their educations.

For the first time in our history, there is a reversal of the trend that tended to reduce the differences in quality between private and public colleges, and between the large and small universities.

If the reversal continues, there will be major differences in the quality of education available at various colleges and universities in the coming years.

Such differences already exist at the primary and secondary school levels.

ASSUMPTION 3:
"Our children can get through college the way we did."

There is literally no chance that our children will be able to pay their own way through college with a combination of part-time jobs and a few small government loans.

College costs are rising too fast.

ASSUMPTION 4:
"We can figure out how to pay for college later."

Maybe. But probably not.

Average incomes are increasing slower than the rate of inflation.

College costs are rising faster than the rate of inflation.

And private college costs are increasing faster than public college costs.

It is more difficult than ever to save enough to pay for an expensive college.

It will be virtually impossible for today's young children to work their way through college.

And a student who has to borrow the money for college will incur a financial burden that will disrupt his or her life for many years.

A child born in 1990 will have to pay from $45,000 to $60,000 for four years at a public university, $100,000 for four years at a private college, and as much as $250,000 for four years at an Ivy League college!

ASSUMPTION 5:
"A college degree is a four-year commitment."

Recent studies show that fewer than 15 percent of today's students get their degrees in four years. Fewer than half graduate in six years!

In other words, more than half of today's students will take seven years or more to get a "four-year" degree.

Therefore, the real cost of a future college education will not be four times the expected annual cost. It could be as much as six or seven times the projected cost of a year in college.

You can almost double the estimates on the previous page.

Of course, some students that take more than four years to receive their degrees are working while going to college part time. In those cases annual tuition and expenses will be lower than for full-time students.

ASSUMPTION 6:

"College costs are the only reason to save for our children."

That was the case a few years ago. But no longer.

Our children are going to need a "grub stake" as they venture out into tomorrow's world.

"Need" is probably too strong a word.

But having some financial help is going to make a big difference to our children.

The three most common things that young adults need help with are:

1) College
2) A Car
3) A downpayment on a home.

ASSUMPTION 7:

"I can't save enough to pay for a fancy college. So it's not worth doing anything."

Nothing could be farther from the truth!

Even if your children have to figure out their own ways to pay for college, think of what it would mean if you had a little money put away to give them some help when they need it.

What would it feel like if you could help them with a down payment on a house?

What if you could buy or help them buy a car?

What if you could treat them to a vacation when they really need one?

What if you could pick up the hospital and doctor bills for their child--your grandchild?

This is not just a save-for-college book. It is a handbook of basic saving and investing.

One of the most important reasons to save and invest for your children is to help them through college. This book will help you do that.

But I hope everyone who reads this book understands that our world is changing faster than most of us expected. Year by year, it is becoming more important to have some financial backing in all areas of our lives, whether or not college is part of the plan.

It is clear that the financial needs of our children are, and will be, far greater than the needs we had.

But there is another "need " I want to discuss. It is the need for this book.

That probably sounds a little self-serving. And I suppose it is. But while I was reviewing my research files, I ran across an article that threw me off balance for a while.

It was an article by a financial writer who claimed that the two "best" investments for a child's account were tax-free bonds and common stocks.

His argument was based on the somewhat complicated tax structure that applies to investment earnings by children. We will look at taxes in a minute. But first, I want to explain why his advice caught me off guard.

His argument was that because of the current tax laws, there is a benefit to be gained from investing in assets that are either tax-free or that appreciate in value, thereby putting off tax liabilities until your child is older.

When I reread his article, which I had clipped from a newspaper some time ago, I thought: "This guy seems to make sense. What are people going to think when I tell them to use zero-coupon Treasury bonds as one of the basic investments in their child's portfolio?"

So I decided I had better take a minute to explain my position.

After all, if you are reading this book, you are probably going to read all sorts of advice. And a lot of it will seem to make sense.

But one of the major purposes of this book is to help you judge that advice. So I want to be as clear as possible.

It is true that there are tax-avoidance reasons for choosing stocks or tax-free bonds instead of zero-coupon bonds. But there are other--more important--reasons for choosing zero-coupon Treasury bonds.

I have three objections to tax-free bonds. One is that tax-free bonds are not risk free. The second is that it takes more money to buy them. The third is that normal tax-free bonds pay annual dividends, which means they do not offer compound interest. (There are some tax-free zero coupon bonds available, but they also carry some risk.)

When you buy U.S. Treasury bonds, there is no question that you will get paid at maturity. The U.S. government is not going to default on its bonds. But tax-free bonds are issued by municipalities. And there have been cases where such bonds were not redeemed at full value. Although the risk of default may be small, it is real. And I am not comfortable with that risk--not for the investments that make up the foundation for your child's financial future.

Secondly, when you buy zero-coupon Treasury bonds, you buy them at a "deep discount." You can pay a couple hundred dollars for a zero-coupon bond that will be worth $1,000 at maturity. Normal bonds--tax-free or not--are bought at face value (or at a small discount, depending upon market interest rates.) In other words, you can purchase a zero-coupon Treasury bond with your shoe-box money. But you need somewhere around $1,000 to buy a regular bond.

Thirdly, when you purchase bonds that pay annual or semi-annual dividends, you do not automatically earn compound interest on your investment. For example, if a tax-free bond pays six percent interest, you will receive $60 per year for each $1,000 bond you buy. That is a six percent return on your $1,000. But you then have to do something with all the $60 dividends.

You do not automatically earn interest on your interest--which is what compound interest is all about. You do not lock in compound interest for the life of the bond.

And the earnings on the reinvested interest will not be tax-free, unless they can be reinvested in additional tax-free bonds.

I have similar reservations about common stocks.

If I knew I could invest in common stocks that would appreciate in value over the years, stocks would be a great way to build wealth while also avoiding some taxes.

But stocks are not a guaranteed investment.

Therefore, choosing stocks means gambling with your child's future. And unless you are wealthy enough to not worry about losing a substantial part of your investment, I do not think the small tax savings can compensate for the known risk.

You may avoid some taxes. But you could end up with nothing in the end.

That is why I believe zero-coupon Treasury bonds are one of the best investments for a child's portfolio.

We will examine stocks and bonds later. And we will see that they can make a lot of sense, under the right circumstances.

But I do not believe they should be used as the primary investments in the typical child's portfolio.

And I hope that one of the "needs" this book will fill is the need to keep the mountains of "advice" in perspective.

But before we look more closely at the investment opportunities available, I want to explain one of the most misunderstood parts of the whole process of saving and investing for children:

What are the tax consequences of giving money to our children?

Giving Money to Children

As soon as you decide to do more than save and invest birthday money and extra cash, you need a bigger or more "sophisticated" shoe box.

If you want to add hundreds or thousands of dollars to your child's portfolio each year, you do not want to do it by cashing checks and putting the money in a shoe box.

For one thing, your young children might think they discovered some long-lost treasure and go on a spending spree.

More importantly, money sitting in a shoe box is not earning interest.

So you need more. You need an account that is safe (insured), that pays interest as soon as the money is deposited, and that lets you invest the funds in other assets without withdrawing them.

There are two standard choices: a trust fund and a custodial account (a Uniform Gift to Minors account[*]).

But before we look at these accounts, each of which can be opened at a bank, brokerage firm, or many mutual funds, let us first see what tax concerns cover our "gifts" to our children.

---

[*] In some states, such as Minnesota, Montana, and North Dakota, these custodial accounts exist under the "Uniform Transfers to Minors Act" Statute.

Gift Tax

The tax law says that anyone can give anyone else up to $10,000 each year without generating a gift tax. You do not even have to report the gift to the IRS.

Each parent can give each child as much as $10,000 a year without incurring gift taxes and without filling out any special tax forms. Two parents--married, separated, or divorced--can give each child as much as $20,000 per year.

Grandparents can do the same. Each grandparent can give each grandchild up to $10,000 a year with no gift-tax consequences.

For most of us, that is probably more than we can afford to do in most years.

And because of the current income-tax law, you may not want to transfer more than that to your child's account anyway.

In fact, you may not want to put even that much money under your child's eventual control, which is what happens with either a custodial account or trust fund.

If you want to transfer more than $10,000 ($20,000 for two parents) to a child's account each year, you could pay a stiff gift tax.

And if you pay a gift tax, it means paying double taxes on your earnings--income taxes when you earn the money and gift taxes when you give it to your children.

That is why it is normally better to stay within the limits that avoid gift taxes.

Gift-tax rates range from 18 percent for gifts just above $10,000 to 49 percent for gifts over $2,000,000.

If you make a taxable gift of $60,000, for example, the tax would be $13,000. And in case you are not aware of the way gift taxes work, it is you, not the recipient, who is responsible for paying the tax.

However--and this is a big however--according to the IRS, if you are a U.S. citizen or resident, you can "use the unified credit to reduce any gift tax for which you may be liable."

What is the "unified credit?" It is a deduction that lets you give much more than $10,000 to a child (or anyone else) in any year without paying a gift tax.

In fact, because of the unified credit, you may not have to worry about gift taxes at all.

The unified credit is a lifetime exemption of $192,000 against gift taxes incurred after 1987.

Here is how it works.

Assume that you make a $160,000 gift to your child in one year.

According to the Unified Rate Schedule (the gift tax rates), the tax on $150,000 ($160,000 minus the $10,000 exemption) is $38,800. In other words, after giving your child $160,000, it looks like you also have to give the IRS $38,800.

But that is not the case.

The actual calculation is as follows:

Total gift:	$160,000
Minus: Annual exclusion:	10,000
Taxable gift:	$150,000
Plus: Prior taxable gifts:	0
Total taxable gifts:	$150,000
Gift tax before unified credit:	$38,800
Minus: Allowable unified credit:	38,800
Net gift tax:	0

Over your lifetime you can use the unified credit exemption to reduce your gift taxes by as much as $192,000. For someone in a 32 percent tax bracket, that means being able to give a total tax-free gift of $600,000.

The item in the above table labeled: "Prior taxable gifts" is zero in our example. But if you had previously (in prior years) given other taxable gifts (more than the annual exclusion), you would enter the total of all taxable gifts on that line. You would then calculate the "tentative tax on total taxable gifts" (adding up all the taxable gifts over the years and computing the total tax on that sum). After subtracting taxes paid on any prior taxable gifts, you get a total gift tax figure. If that figure is less than $192,000 minus any previous unified credit exemptions used, you will not have to pay any gift taxes.

But remember, this is a "lifetime" exclusion.

Each year's calculations take account of allowable unified credits used in the past. And the *total* cannot exceed $192,000.

But the important point is that you can give your children more than $10,000 in a given year without paying a gift tax.

It is commonly believed that if you exceed the $10,000 per year exclusion, you will have to pay a gift tax. That is not true.

If your gifts are less than $10,000 per-year per-person, you do not have to report them to the IRS. If you go beyond the limit, you have to report the gifts. But because of the unified credit, you still will not pay a tax. You will, however, have to fill out the correct forms.

Simply ask the IRS for a unified credit form.

But before you take advantage of every possibility for transferring money to a child's name, there are arguments against switching large sums into a child's account.

One is that expenditures on medical expenses and tuition are not considered to be gifts. So you can spend an unlimited amount of money on your child's education or medical expenses without paying any gift taxes. The money must be paid directly to the institution. And if it is for education, it applies only to tuition. According to the IRS: "It does not apply to books, supplies, dormitory fees, etc."

In other words, if you pay for your child's tuition, the money is not counted as part of the $10,000 per year tax-free gift. And it does not affect the $192,000 unified credit exemption.

Therefore, if you pay your child's tuition directly to the institution, there is no gift tax to worry about, even if it ends up being as much as $40,000 to $100,000 per year. In fact, you can still give your child another $10,000 to $20,000 (two parents) as an annual tax-free gift.

And because of the unified credit discussed above, you can use your own funds to pay for all other college expenses without incurring a gift tax--even if they exceed the $10,000 to $20,000 limit--as long as you have not used up your unified credits by that time.

Very simply, there is little reason to beat the gift tax.

Your children can work for you

Another way to "give" money to children without having it counted as part of the $10,000 per-person per-year exclusion is to have your children work for you.

You have to be either self employed or run a profitable part-time business. But if you are or do, you should know that you can hire your children to do real work for you.

You do not want to fool around with the IRS by cooking up a phoney job and then paying your child a "salary" that is really a gift. In most cases, it is not necessary to "beat" the gift tax. You and your spouse together can give your child up to $20,000 per year anyway. And because of the unified credit, you can actually transfer hundreds of thousands of dollars to your child without a gift tax. In most cases, that's more than enough.

But if you have a business and you want your children to work for you, here is what you should know.

1) You do not have to pay your children the minimum wage. The issue of how much you can pay your own children was fought in the courts. And it was decided that you are free to pay your children a "fair" wage--a wage that is comparable to what you would have to pay someone else. You have to take account of the fact that your children may be younger and have less experience that a "comparable" employee. But you can pay them a real wage for answering the phone, filing, cleaning, typing, doing research, taking care of the mail, and so on.

2) You can deduct the wages you pay your children as a legitimate business expense. Therefore, you can transfer the tax burden on that income from you to your children.

3) If your child is under fourteen years of age, he or she may have to pay taxes at your tax rate. We will see why in the next section: "The 'Kiddie' Tax."

4) If your child is fourteen or older, he or she will pay taxes at his or her rate--not yours.

So if you have a legitimate business--full or part time--and you want your children to work with you, there can be a tax advantage. Their wages are not part of the annual tax-free gift. And you can deduct what you pay them as a business expense.

Plus--your children learn the value of work. And they get to work with their parents.

Giving money to children--summary

The main points of this section are:

* You can transfer a lot of money to your children without incurring a gift tax--$10,000 per person, per year to each child. Grandparents can do so as well.

* If you give more, you may have to pay a stiff gift tax.

* But because of the lifetime unified credit, you can actually transfer an additional $600,000 in gifts (in total).

* Money spent directly on your child's tuition or medical expenses is not a taxable gift, no matter how much it is.

* In most cases, there is no real tax advantage in transferring a lot of money to a young child's account. And there can be a potential danger.

Most importantly, as we will see in the next section, the major reasons for thinking carefully before transferring as much money as the gift tax allows are:

1) The income-tax advantages of making investments in your child's name are slight.

2) In order to get even the minimal tax advantages now available, the gift to your child must be irrevocable. Once the money is transferred to your child's account, it belongs to the child.

Conclusion

The lifetime unified credit means that most of us do not have to worry about gift taxes. We will not go over the limit.

But being able to give all you can afford to give without paying a gift tax is only one issue.

You still have to decide how much money you want to have--or should have--invested in a child's account. And how much should be kept in your name or your spouse's name.

To make that decision, you have to understand the "Kiddie" tax and the advantages and disadvantages of custodial accounts and trust funds, which is our next section.

Taxes, Custodial Accounts, and Trust Funds

The major reason for having a custodial account or a trust fund is to let you make investments in your child's name.

And one of the major reasons for making investments in your child's name is to gain a tax advantage *for your child.*

In the past, you could gain a tax advantage *for yourself* by transferring funds into a child's account, making investments that would be taxed at the child's lower rate, and then switching the money back into your name.

But Congress decided that people--especially wealthy parents--were taking advantage of a loophole in the tax law. And in 1986 a new tax law was passed.

The new law changed two important features:

1) Tax rates on children's accounts were increased.

2) All transfers or gifts made to either a custodial account or a trust fund are now *irrevocable*--which means once the money is transferred to the child's account, it is the child's money. Period. The parents cannot take the money back without paying a stiff penalty.

As a result of these two changes, custodial accounts and trust funds offer both smaller advantages and greater dangers.

Custodial accounts

A custodial account is exactly what it sounds like.

It is an account in your child's name with you or another adult named as custodian.

You can open a custodial account at a brokerage firm, bank, or mutual fund.

All you need is a Social Security number for your child and a few minutes to take care of the paperwork.

The advantages of such an account are clear:

- It is an easy place to deposit your shoe-box money and any other money you transfer to your child on a regular or irregular basis.
- The investments are in the child's name.
- Any money deposited will automatically earn competitive short-term interest rates.
- It is easy to switch from interest-bearing assets to other assets, such as stocks, bonds, etc.
- There is a small tax advantage if your child is under fourteen years of age.
- There is a large tax advantage when your child is fourteen or older.
- If someone other than yourself is listed as the custodian, the funds in the account are not considered to be part of your estate. Therefore, the funds can avoid probate. I consider this to be a marginal advantage, however, and recommend that you and your spouse be listed as joint custodians.
- There are normally no fees for such accounts.

The disadvantages of custodial accounts are as clear as their advantages:

- The tax break for children under fourteen years old is small.
- All the money put into such accounts is an "irrevocable" gift to the child.

You cannot give money to a child by putting it in a custodial account and then take the money back later. If you do, you will be hit with a large penalty.

For most of us, once we give money to our children, we are not going to think about taking it back again anyway.

But there are two things to consider.

One is that you might need the money more than your children at some time in the future.

The other is that as soon as your child reaches the "age of majority" (18 to 21 years old, depending upon state law), he or she can bring a birth certificate to your broker or banker and withdraw all the funds.

Looking at a three-month old baby asleep in a crib, the last thing you would worry about is that he or she might "squander" your savings. But if you look at 16- or 17-year olds, you may decide that you have a reason to be cautious.

There is a definite tax advantage in letting funds accumulate in a child's name--especially after the child turns fourteen. But the savings come at a cost--you do not maintain control of the money.

Trust funds

If you live in a state where your child does not reach the age of majority until 21, it is possible that you will spend all, or most, of the funds in a custodial account on college expenses before the child takes control.

An alternative is to set up a trust fund.

Unfortunately:

- Trust funds are more complicated than custodial accounts.
- Unlike the trust funds of the past, today's do not offer any great tax advantages.
- Trust funds can be expensive to establish.
- Like a custodial account, trust funds require an irrevocable gift--once the funds are put into a trust fund, they belong to the child.

The main advantage of a trust fund is that it can give you more control over how the funds are used.

By paying an attorney to set up a trust fund, you can specify how and when the assets will be distributed to the child. But the attorney's fee can be as much as $1,500, or more, depending upon how detailed you want to get.

There are no "rules" for trust funds. Each is a separate and unique legal entity. That is why they are expensive to set up.

And if you have a bank act as trustee, the bank will most likely charge you an annual fee plus a percentage of the account's total value. It is common for a bank to charge $500 per year plus one percent of the fund's value.

Taxes

Taxes are one of the primary reasons for establishing custodial accounts and trust funds.

But if you are going to make an irrevocable gift to your children, thereby giving up eventual control of the money or having to pay an attorney to maintain some control, what are you or your children getting in return? What are you saving on taxes?

Custodial Accounts

Taxes on unearned income (investment income) are:
For children under age 14 (the "Kiddie" tax):

- The first $500 is exempt.
- The next $500 is taxed at 15 percent.
- All investment income over $1,000 is taxed at the parents' highest rate. If the parents file separately, for any reason, the child pays whatever the parent with the highest rate must pay.

For children 14 and older:

- The first $3,100 is tax free.
- The next $18,550 is taxed at 15 percent.
- Anything over $21,650 is taxed at 28 percent.

When the child has earned income as well, the calculations get a little messy.

But the easiest way to think of taxes on custodial accounts is that the income is taxed at the parents' rate (after the $1,000 deduction) until the child is 14 years of age.

After 14, the income is taxed at the child's rate.

But remember, the IRS considers you to reach a given age on the day *before* your birthday. So if your child was born on January 1, he or she is considered to be 14 for the previous year.

What does the current tax schedule mean?

It means that as long as your child is younger than 14, once you have accumulated enough money in a custodial account to yield at least $1,000 a year in income, every additional dollar you add to that account generates income that will be taxed at your rate.

Therefore, if your child is under age 14, there is no tax advantage in transferring large sums of money to a custodial account. Neither you nor the child gets a tax break.

Of course, if you use the funds in a custodial account to purchase stocks, or any other appreciating asset, the tax liability is put off until the stocks are sold, which can be after the child turns 14. In that case, the profits are taxed at the child's rate, which is a true advantage.

That is why many analysts recommend stocks for a child's account, rather than bonds that generate yearly dividend income. However, as I explained previously, although stocks offer the opportunity to defer taxes, they do not offer a guaranteed profit.

Besides, if you want to invest in stocks, you can buy them in your name and wait until your child is 14 before transferring them to a custodial account.

You get the same tax break if the stock was held for years in a custodial account or in your name.

Trust Fund Taxes

The tax rates on trust funds are independent of a child's age, and of the parents' tax bracket.

- The first $5,000 of income is taxed at 15 percent.
- The next $8,000 at 28 percent.
- The next $13,000 at 33 percent.
- Everything above $26,000 is taxed at 28 percent.

As you can see, the taxes on income in a custodial account are lower than the taxes on the same income in a trust fund--if the child is age 14 or older.

But for a child under age 14, the better tax deal is a function of the annual earnings. For example, if you have $10,000 invested at 10 percent interest, the annual income is $1,000.

If the money is in a custodial account, and you are in the 28 percent marginal tax bracket:

$500 is tax free.

$500 is taxed at 15 percent.

And the total tax is $75.

If the money is in a trust fund, the entire $1,000 is taxed at a 15 percent rate, which is $150.

So for smaller levels of investment income, taxes are lower on a custodial account. Plus, you have to pay to set up the trust fund and possibly to cover the cost of a trustee.

Because of the different tax schedules, it is normally assumed that a trust is better than a custodial account only if it has a value of $50,000 to $60,000.

But the tax savings must be weighed against the cost of setting up and administering a trust.

If you have $60,000 invested at 10 percent interest in a custodial account, the $6,000 in income will incur a tax of $1,475.

($500 tax free, $500 at 15 percent, and $5,000 at 28 percent--if that is your tax rate.)

If the $60,000 were in a trust fund instead, the total tax would be $1,030.

($5,000 at 15 percent, and $1,000 at 28 percent.)

So the taxes on the trust are lower by $445, which is a large savings--if there are no trust expenses.

However, as the value of the account increases, the tax savings remain about the same.

For example, assume you have $100,000 invested at 10 percent interest. That is an annual income of $10,000.

In a custodial account, the taxes would be $2,520.

($500 tax free, $500 at 15 percent, and $5,000 at 28 percent--if you are in the 28 percent tax bracket.)

In a trust fund, the tax would be $2,150.

(15 percent of $5,000--which is $750--plus 28 percent of the next $5,000--which is $1,400.)

The tax savings on the trust fund are $370.

But if you pay a bank $500 a year plus one percent of the fund's value ($1,000 in this case), your actual after-tax return is reduced by another $1,500. As a result, the taxes-plus-expenses total is higher for the trust fund: $3,650 versus $2,520.

Of course, if you manage the trust yourself, with no expenses, you can come out ahead.

If you do decide to set up a trust, the simplest and least expensive is a "minor's trust." If you find the right attorney, the initial cost could be only a few hundred dollars. But you will still have more tax forms to deal with each year; the tax savings are not what you might have expected; and the money still belongs to the child, although most of it may be spent during college, before the fund is turned over to the child at age 21 (which is the case with a minor's trust).

A sensible plan

If you got bored with the numbers we just went through, let me summarize what it all means.

1) Money transferred to a custodial account or trust fund is an irrevocable gift. It is the child's money when the child reaches age 18 or 21. (The age can be extended for certain, more expensive, trusts.)

2) For children under age 14, custodial accounts offer a tax break on the first $1,000 of unearned income.

3) Unearned income over $1,000 a year is taxed at the parents' rate if the child is under age 14.

4) For children under age 14, there is no clear-cut tax advantage in setting up a trust fund.

5) For children 14 and older, taxes are lower on custodial accounts than trust funds--without question.

6) But any tax savings must be weighed against the fact that with a custodial account, the child can do whatever he or she wants to do with the money at age 18 or 21.

7) Therefore, the major advantage of a trust fund is to maintain some control over how and when the money is distributed to the child.

Given what we now know, here is a sensible way of dealing with the current laws:

- After your child is born, open a custodial account at a brokerage firm, bank, or mutual fund. Talk with each to see which you are most comfortable with. Some offer better monthly statements. Some offer a wider range of investment options. But if you intend to stick with standard financial assets (stocks and bonds), you will probably not need an account that lets you make riskier investments.

- As long as your child is under 14 years of age, add money to the custodial account until the annual income reaches $1,000.

- Once the annual income in a custodial account for a child under age 14 reaches $1,000, it does not matter if additional investments are made in the child's name or your name. If the investments yield annual interest or dividends, the interest or dividends above $1,000 will be taxed at your rate, whether the investments are in your name or your child's custodial account. If the investments are in appreciating assets (i.e. stocks), they can be held until the child is 14--either in a custodial account or in your own account.

- Therefore, as soon as you accumulate somewhere around $10,000 to $12,000 in interest-bearing assets in a custodial account, you may want to open a separate account in your name or your spouse's name--a joint account is normally best. Use this new account to continue saving and investing for your child.

- When your child turns 14 (or anytime during the year in which he or she will turn 14), you can transfer assets you are holding in your name into your child's custodial account.
- The reason for transferring funds from your account to your child's account when the child turns 14 is that the income will then be taxed at the much lower child's rate. Until the child turns 14, the tax on investment income greater than $1,000 is the same, no matter whose name the investments are held in.
- Once your child reaches age 14, there is a valid tax-reason to make investments through a custodial account.
- And because of the lifetime unified deduction, you can transfer relatively large sums of money or assets to your child after he or she reaches age 14 without paying a gift tax. Therefore, you can accumulate assets in your name and transfer them to your child at age 14 or older.
- If you expect to accumulate $50,000 to $60,000 while your child is very young, check with your attorney to see about opening a trust fund. Your particular circumstances may make a trust fund a good choice.
- In any case, if you want to build a child's account that reaches $200,000 or $300,000, you will probably want to use a trust fund in order to keep control of the distribution of money. When you are considering making that much money available to an 18 year old, I think there is a legitimate reason to be cautious.

The above plan is based on the current tax law. It lets you take advantage of the tax breaks that now exist.

But behind this plan is another concern--the desire to maintain some control over the money you want to give to your children.

When your children are young--under age 14--there is no tax advantage in accumulating more than about $10,000 to $12,000 in a custodial account. If that much money is invested in interest-bearing assets, that is all you need to reach the $1,000 tax-break limit.

And if you intend to invest in stocks, there is really no advantage to using a custodial account to purchase stocks--either before or after your child is 14.

If your child is under 14, you can buy stocks in your name and transfer them to a custodial account later.

Even after your child turns 14, you can continue to buy stocks in your name and then transfer the ones you want to give your child into a custodial account before selling them.

The tax break comes by selling the stocks through a custodial account, not by holding them in the account.

But why wait?

Why not put as much money as possible into a custodial account just to know your kids will have it?

Because they might not have it. At least, they might not have it to use the way you hope it will be used.

I think it is a mistake to work and sacrifice to build an account that could be "misused" by an 18 year old.

And because there is no tax advantage to do so, why do it?

Why not accumulate the funds in your name and transfer them when your child reaches age 14? By then, you will have a better idea of what your child's goals are. You will have a better idea of how much you can afford to give to your child. You will have a better idea of how much money you think you can trust to your child's eventual discretion.

And if you decide to invest in stocks or other appreciating assets, they can be transferred when your child is even older. Simply transfer the assets before you sell them. That way, the profits will be taxed at the child's lower rate, even if you owned them for many years.

A complete plan

Here is a 12-step outline of a complete financial plan for your children.

1) Get a shoe box to collect gift money and "extra" cash.

2) Open an account for your child with either you or your spouse as custodian -- a custodial account. You will need a Social Security number for your child. So call your local Social Security office for instructions. Basically, all you need to bring is a birth certificate.

3) Transfer your shoe-box money into the custodial account where it will earn insured interest.

4) Use some of your shoe-box money or extra cash to purchase Series EE savings bonds (in your name). The interest is tax-free if used for education. But your adjusted net income will have to be below a certain level to qualify. Currently, the limit is $60,000.

5) Use money in the custodial account to purchase zero-coupon Treasury bonds whenever interest rates are relatively high. You will have to declare the annual "phantom" interest on these bonds as income. But because the bonds start out with a market value of a few hundred dollars, the annual interest grows over time as the bonds gain in value. Therefore, by the time the interest accumulation is fairly large, your child may be 14 or older.

6) While your child is under age 14, there is no reason to let the annual income in the custodial account go above $1,000. If it does go over $1,000 a year, don't worry. Any income over $1,000 will be taxed the same, whether it is in the custodial account or in your name.

7) Open an investment account (a cash-management account is a good choice) in your or your spouse's name (a joint account is best). Or keep careful records of investments made in your name that you will eventually transfer to your child.

8) Make additional contributions—from your shoe box and from regular or irregular transfers--to your new account. You can use an existing account, but if you do, make certain you keep the assets separate—which are yours and which "belong" to your children.

9) As the money in the new account grows, invest it in other assets. Again, I believe zero-coupon Treasury bonds should be the standard--the investment to beat.

10) In the year your child turns 14 (and the following years), you can decide how much you want to transfer from your name to your child's custodial account.

11) Transferring assets to a child age 14 or older means that the income on those investments will be taxed at a lower rate.

12) Remember, however, the money transferred to a custodial account is an irrevocable gift. Therefore, you have to trust your child's ability to make decisions. If you live in a state where the child cannot take control of the funds until age 21, there is less to worry about. By then a large part of the account may have been used to pay for college expenses.

If you want to transfer large sums of money to a child, you should establish a trust fund. Not for the tax advantages. But to maintain more control over the distribution of money.

Summary

If you follow the plan just discussed, you will:

- Keep your shoe box. And keep filling it with gift money and "extra" cash.
- Open a custodial account, but set a limit of $1,000 a year in earnings while your child is under age 14.
- When the custodial account is generating $1,000 a year in income, open an investment account in your name to accumulate additional assets for your child. Or keep track of investments purchased in your name.
- Make regular (or irregular, if necessary) contributions to the custodial account or your account.
- When your child reaches age 14, you can transfer assets from your name to the custodial account to take advantage of the lower tax rates.
- But be aware of the fact that the money in a custodial account is your child's money. At age 18 or 21, he or she can use it for any purpose.
- Therefore, you may be better off paying higher taxes and keeping the funds under your control.
- If you want to build a large portfolio, you should protect yourself and your child by setting up a trust fund.
- And remember--money spent directly on tuition is not considered a taxable gift, no matter how much it is.

Summary of basic investments

Our basic plan is dictated by the tax laws. But the investments are up to us.

I believe that unless you are very wealthy, you should begin by choosing risk-free investments for your children.

Later, as your child's account grows in value, you may want to add some risk in the hopes of earning a greater return.

Until then, I think the best choices are:

1) The insured interest offered in custodial accounts, money market funds, or cash-management accounts at brokerage firms.

2) Zero-coupon Treasury bonds. They are worth the trouble of dealing with the annual tax liability on their "phantom" interest--the interest you do not receive, but which adds to the bond's value each year and must be reported as income.

3) Series EE savings bonds. If you are pretty sure the money will be used for education and if you do not think the income limit will be a problem, these bonds are a good choice. In any case, the worst that can happen is that you, or your child, will have to pay taxes on the interest. And as we will see, because the interest on Series EE bonds accumulates without an annual tax burden, the eventual after-tax return is equal to what you would earn on an investment that pays a higher return but which is taxable annually.

Basic Investments

I believe that your child's financial plan is so important that it should not contain any risk. More accurately, it should contain the smallest possible chance of loss.

The purpose of your child's account is so crucial that the potential rewards from winning on a risky investment are not likely to outweigh the consequences of losing.

Two exceptions are:

· If you are wealthy enough so that your future plans will not be affected by significant losses.

· If the total portfolio value exceeds the projected future needs of your children.

But before I give you a misleading impression of "no risk," let me explain what I mean.

First, risk is a relative, not an absolute, concept. There are no absolutely risk-free investments.

An investment with a guaranteed return of principal and interest means you will not lose your money. But it does not mean you are guaranteed to beat inflation.

So the idea of risk must be handled carefully.

Some people are more afraid of inflation than of the possibility of losing their funds in an investment that turns sour. They believe that the most risk-free investments are precious metals or other "tangible" assets whose prices tend to rise with the rate of inflation.

My belief is that the possibility of being hurt by an unexpected runaway inflation is much smaller than the possibility of losing money on gold, silver, or even a major "blue chip" stock.

At the same time, it is unlikely that inflation will be completely eliminated in the foreseeable future. Therefore, your plans should account for an almost certain four to five percent rate of inflation.

Second, being "risk free" does not mean earning a poor return.

In fact, the future value of your total portfolio will probably be greater if you make only investments that "can't lose" rather than hitting some winners and discarding some losers.

Third, once you have built your child's portfolio to a level that is expected to meet your future "needs," you may decide to add some riskier investments that offer potentially higher returns.

That is fine. My only reservation is that when you invest in assets that can lose as well as gain value, it is not easy to be successful.

It is one thing to say, "OK, now it's time to make some real money." It is another to actually do it.

Obviously, the decision is up to you.

But I want to make two strong recommendations:

1) Keep your child's account as risk free as possible, at least until it reaches a relatively high total value.

2) Even after building a successful portfolio for your child, think carefully before jumping into a "great deal" with "unlimited potential."

What is a relatively high value for a child's portfolio?

That is an individual decision. It depends upon your expected future needs (what the funds will be used for) and upon your total wealth (the wealthier you are, the more risk you can afford).

It is often believed that one way to become wealthier is through investing. Sometimes that will happen.

But a child's account is not the place to try to improve your wealth position. It should be a place to do the best you can for your children, within your abilities.

"Risk-free" investments

Money market mutual funds, Certificates of Deposit, zero-coupon Treasury bonds, Series EE savings bonds, and regular Treasury bonds, notes, and bills are some of the most risk-free opportunities available.

Each is either issued by the United States government or insured by a trustworthy source. Therefore, you know you will get your money back--with interest.

That is why I believe such investments should make up the lion's share your child's portfolio.

But as I have already explained, whenever you put your money into a long-term, interest-bearing asset, you may have to worry about inflation. Buying a long-term government bond that pays nine percent interest may sound great when the inflation rate is two to three percent. But if inflation soars to ten or eleven percent, your money will be losing value each year. The purchasing power of your investment will decline day by day. And if you want to sell before maturity, you will probably have to take a loss.

More importantly, because no one should make investments they do not understand, I want to take a few minutes to explain the above options.

To begin with, all investments can be separated into either "own" or "loan" categories.

When you make an investment, you are either buying ownership of an asset, which may give you a share of future profits, or making a loan to someone.

If you buy gold or stocks or part of an oil well, you are hoping that the value of what you "own" will increase over time. If it is gold, you hope that the price of gold will rise. If it is a stock, you hope that the price of that particular stock will increase. If it is a share in an oil well, you hope that your cut of future profits will be greater than your investment. (I am not going to discuss "tax-advantaged" investments in oil wells, or any other schemes designed to beat the IRS. The new tax laws virtually eliminated those tax breaks. Today, you have to make investments that return real profits--not tax write-offs.)

When you buy "debt instruments," such as bonds or CDs, you are actually making a loan. When you buy a bond or CD, it means that someone is borrowing money from you. In return, they promise to pay back the loan plus interest. In some cases, the interest you receive is fixed. In others, it varies over time.

Sometimes you receive interest payments on an annual or semi-annual basis (e.g. regular bonds and notes).

Sometimes all the interest accumulates and is paid to you when the asset reaches maturity (e.g. zero-coupon bonds, CDs, Series EE savings bonds).

And sometimes the life of the asset is so short that even though all the interest is due at maturity, it seems as though you are constantly being paid (e.g. three-month Treasury bills).

There is, however, one thing that all these investments have in common. None offers any collateral.

Of course, collateral does not guarantee that a lender will not lose money. Using a house as collateral for a mortgage cannot protect a bank's total investment if real estate prices fall.

That is why it is normally better to loan money to someone you can "trust," such as the United States government, or to a borrower who is insured by a responsible agency. More important than collateral is knowing, without a doubt, you will be paid.

But what are the best choices?

What is the difference between bonds, notes, and bills?

And why are some people afraid to invest in bonds?

A few questions and answers

Q: Who issues bonds, notes, and bills?

A: Anyone who wants to borrow money. Not individuals. But corporations, municipalities, public utilities, school districts, counties, states, the federal government, and federal agencies.

Q: Why borrow money?

A: To meet current expenses, or to expand.

Corporations can raise money in three ways: take it from retained earnings (if they have any), sell stock (which gives up some ownership of the company), or borrow (sell bonds). Part of an owner's or manager's job is to decide which method is best. Sometimes, the best choice is to borrow.

State and local governments have two choices: raise taxes or borrow--sell bonds.

The federal government can also raise taxes or sell bonds. But it has a third choice. In conjunction with the Federal Reserve Bank, the federal government can create new money to meet its current expenses.

If the government is worried that raising taxes will cause an economic slowdown and that creating new money might result in inflation, it will borrow a large part of the money it needs by selling bonds, notes, and bills.

Q: What is the difference between bonds, notes, and bills?

A: The time to maturity when they are originally issued.

Treasury bills are issued to come due in three, six, or twelve months.

Treasury notes are issued to mature in one to ten years.

Bonds are issued to mature in ten to thirty years.

Q: Do you have to hold a bond or note until maturity?

A: No. Almost all bills, notes, and bonds are marketable, which means they can be sold to someone else after their initial purchase. You can buy a 30-year bond and sell it whenever you want. You cannot normally sell it back to the issuer until maturity. But you can sell it to another investor.

You can also purchase a 20-year bond that was originally issued 15-years ago, which means it will mature in only five years. If you hold it until maturity, it will be redeemed at face value (normally $1,000 or $5,000) by the issuing agency or corporation. If you want to sell it before it reaches maturity, you can do that as well. You can buy and sell bonds, notes, and bills whenever you want.

As a result, you can purchase 30-year bonds that will mature at any times you choose--in 18-years, 19-years, or whatever.

But whatever you purchase, it will stop earning interest on the original maturity date.

Q: Is there any advantage to purchasing original issues?

A: Not unless you want to lock in current interest rates for as long as possible. Then you would buy bonds with the longest possible time to maturity, which would be original issues.

Q: Can I always buy and sell bonds at the same price?

A: No. The face value of a bill, note, or bond is what you will receive when the bond is redeemed at maturity. A $1,000 30-year Treasury bond or a $1,000 zero-coupon bond will be worth $1,000 at maturity.

But if you buy or sell such bonds after they are originally issued, the price you pay or receive depends upon current market interest rates. For example, if you buy a new 30-year bond when such bonds are paying nine percent interest, you will pay $1,000 for the bond. And in 30-years, you will get your $1,000 back. In the meantime, you will receive nine percent interest each year, which is $90, until the bond matures or until you sell it.

What happens if market interest rates rise so that new bonds are issued to pay ten percent interest, or $100, a year? Your bond will still pay only $90 a year because when such bonds are issued, the dollar value of the annual interest is fixed at the original level. Therefore, if you want to sell your bond, no one will give you $1,000 for it because for $1,000 they can buy a bond that pays $100 a year instead of $90.

So if you want to sell your bond, you will have to settle for less than $1,000.

Of course, if you hold it until maturity, you will always receive $1,000--no matter what happens to market interest rates.

Q: What is the best way to avoid getting stuck with a loss due to rising interest rates?

A: Buy bonds that you expect to hold until maturity. If you want a bond that you can sell in 19-years (for example, when your one year old will be twenty), buy one that will mature in 19-years. That way, you know exactly what interest you will earn, and you know what the bond will be worth when you sell it.

Do not buy a new 30-year bond and plan on selling it in the open market in 19-years. If you do, you might have to sell it at a loss, which could negate a large part of the interest you earned over the years.

Of course, if interest rates fall after you buy your bond, you can sell for a profit!

Q: How do you get the highest interest?

A: Interest, or yield, is a function of two factors: risk and time to maturity. The greater the risk of possible default, the higher the yield will be. And the longer the time to maturity, the higher the yield will normally be. Sometimes, however, because of economic circumstances, short-term yields can be greater than long-term yields.

Q: When is the interest paid?

A: Treasury bills, Series EE savings bonds, and zero-coupon bonds pay all their interest at maturity. Standard notes and bonds pay interest twice a year.

Q: Which are the "best" bonds and notes to buy?

A: That depends upon a number of factors: yields, risk, expectations of future inflation and interest rates, the size of the investment you want to make, and what makes sense to you. I like zero-coupon Treasury bonds. Some people will not buy them because they refuse to pay yearly taxes on accumulating interest that they will not receive until the bonds mature.

In any case, the choices can be overwhelming. Corporate versus government issues. Taxable government bonds versus tax-free municipal bonds. Short-term versus long-term issues. Interest-bearing bonds versus zero-coupon bonds. Treasury bonds versus government agency bonds. Treasury bills versus money market funds. New issues versus secondary purchases.

Whatever you pick, you can find someone who will argue that it is the best choice, which should not be surprising. Each offers something the others do not. Therefore, each will be "best" for someone. If that were not true, all the choices would not exist. Those that serve no special purpose would disappear from the market because no one would buy them. So if someone tries to tell you that one choice is always best, he is wrong. And if someone tries to tell you that one choice is absolutely worthless, he is wrong too.

If something exists, there is almost always a reason for it to do so. The question is: What is best for a given purpose?

In our case: What is best for your child's account?

In the end, only you can answer that question.

But I can give you my opinion and my reasoning.

For a child's account, my choices are:

1) Zero-coupon Treasury bonds purchased to mature when your child reaches selected ages.

2) Series EE savings bonds purchased to be held at least five years, in order to gain the highest yield they offer.

3) An insured interest-bearing account—a custodial account at a bank, brokerage firm, or mutual fund.

That's it.

They are three of the most risk-free choices.

Plus, they offer good returns.

They make sense, given the current tax law. And each can be purchased for a small price.

It costs at least $1,000 to buy regular notes and bonds. And the minimum price of a new Treasury bill is $10,000.

But zero-coupon Treasury bonds can be bought for two or three hundred dollars (sometimes as little as $100), depending upon interest rates and time to maturity. Series EE savings bonds can be purchased for as little as $25. And interest-bearing accounts can be opened for whatever you have on hand.

Also, regular notes and bonds pay semi-annual dividends instead of compound interest. Therefore, you are always faced with the job of reinvesting the interest. A $1,000 bond at 10 percent interest will pay you a total of $100 a year. And it is not easy to find something to do with $100. (One possibility is to use the interest to buy Series EE savings bonds.)

Of course, if you have $10,000 or $20,000 worth of such bonds, you can use the annual interest to buy more of the same.

Why worry about what to do with the interest on regular notes and bonds? Because that is the return on your investment. If you buy a bond for $1,000, you get your $1,000 back at maturity. The only gain is the annual interest payments. So what you do with that money is crucial to making such bonds a good investment.

In the past, it was common to buy such bonds in order to earn a yearly income that would be spent, not reinvested. That is still, in my opinion, their best use.

Another important question is: Should I buy short-term or long-term interest-bearing investments.

I can explain this one to you, but I cannot give you a simple recommendation. That is because the question of short-term versus long-term depends upon expectations of future interest rates.

If you think interest rates are relatively low (and will be increasing), you do not want to make an investment that locks in the current rate. You do not want to buy zero-coupon bonds or regular long-term bonds. You want to leave your funds in an account that earns short-term rates and let the money be continually reinvested at higher and higher rates. Then, when you think rates are high enough, switch to a long-term investment that will lock-in those yields.

If you think interest rates are relatively high (and will be falling), you want to lock-in the current rate while you can. You want to buy long-term zero-coupon bonds instead of leaving your funds in short-term assets.

Very simply, if you expect interest rates to fall, buy long-term bonds. If you expect interest rates to rise, keep your funds in a money-market account. (That does not mean selling long-term bonds you already own. What we are talking about here is what to do with new money added to an account.)

It sounds simple. But even the top experts have trouble forecasting future interest rates. So never hesitate to talk to your broker and to others to see what they think--and why.

Whenever someone gives you financial advice, always ask: Why?

Q: What about inflation?

A: Inflation is a tricky issue. During periods of rising inflation, interest rates have to increase as well because it makes no sense to let someone else use your money if what you eventually get back will not buy as much as it could have bought when you made the loan.

Therefore, if you buy a long-term bond at a non-inflationary interest rate and then inflation picks up, your bond will be a "bad" investment during the period of inflation. But as inflation cools off, your bond becomes a good investment again.

Many financial advisors forget that we live in a cyclical world. But if you buy a 30-year bond and hold it for 30-years, there will be times when you will be disappointed--because you could have done better. And there will be times when you will be glad.

On the other hand, short-term interest rates--the rates you earn on 3-month Treasury bills, CDs, or money-market funds will almost always be above the inflation rate. These short-term rates have to make sense when the investment is made. Otherwise, no one will buy them.

So if you are afraid of inflation, here is a two-step plan.

1) Leave your money in money-market funds or CDs (the automatic investments for most custodial accounts and cash-management accounts).

2) Do not make any long-term investments until periods of high inflation cause interest rates to rise to very high levels.

Normally, the highest interest rates occur as the money supply is contracted to reduce the inflation rate. So if inflation does become a serious issue, wait until it is clear that the money supply is being restricted. The lower the quantity of money available for loans, the higher interest rates will climb. And that is when you can switch from short-term interest-bearing assets to long-term bonds.

Another way to deal with the possibility of inflation is to choose Series EE savings bonds. If you hold them for more than five years, they pay a variable rate of interest which will almost certainly be greater than the rate of inflation.

Then there are tangible assets, such as gold, silver, and collectibles. Some people believe that our persistent inflation rate makes such investments the best choice of all.

But that is a tough claim to back up. It is easy to find periods of time when gold or silver or certain collectibles outperformed all other investments. The problem is that tangible assets, like stocks, can lose as well as gain value.

And for a child's portfolio, it is hard to beat earning interest that is higher than the rate of inflation. The money just keeps accumulating. For example, if you buy Series EE savings bonds, they can never be worth less than what you paid for them. The same is true of funds in an interest-bearing account.

Q: How can you calculate the return on investments that yield compound interest--such as zero-coupon and Series EE bonds?

A: You can use the "rule of 72" to get a quick answer.

If you divide the number 72 by any interest rate, the answer represents the number of years it will take for your original investment to double in value. Or if you divide the number 72 by any number of years, the answer represents the compound interest rate you would have to receive in order for your original investment to double in that many years.

For example, if the current interest rate on CDs, money-market funds or zero-coupon bonds is eight percent, dividing eight into 72 gives you nine. That means your investment will double in value every nine years.

If you invest $250 at an eight percent compounded annual rate of return, the $250 will be worth $500 in nine years. And in nine more years, it will double again--to $1,000.

That is how zero-coupon bonds appreciate.

Money-market rates work the same--except for the fact that money-market rates change over time while zero-coupon bond rates are locked-in for the life of the bond.

The point is: You can buy a zero-coupon Treasury bond for $250 at eight percent interest and know it will be worth $1,000 in 18 years.

Or you can let the money accumulate in a money-market fund. If rates stay at eight percent, it too will be worth $1,000 in 18 years. If rates rise, it will be worth more. If rates fall, it will be worth less than $1,000.

In each case, however, the annual appreciation or interest must be reported as income--either in your child's name or yours.

Series EE savings bonds are different.

With Series EE bonds, the annual appreciation does not have to be reported as income.

And if the money is used for education, the interest will be totally tax free.

Now before discussing a number of other investment opportunities, I want to give you a little more specific information on our three basic choices: zero-coupon Treasury bonds, Series EE savings bonds, and short-term interest-bearing accounts.

Zero-Coupon Treasury Bonds

Zero-coupon Treasury bonds are U.S. government bonds that do not pay yearly dividends. Instead, they are sold at a "discount"--meaning that the price you pay to buy them is less than the price you receive when they mature. The difference between what you pay and what you receive is the total compounded interest on your investment.

The typical zero-coupon bond has a maturity value of $1,000. That means you receive $1,000 for each bond when it "matures" or comes due.

How much does each bond cost? That depends upon two factors: how long it will be held before it matures, and current interest rates. Zero-coupon bonds that pay a nine percent yield will double in value every eight years. That means you can buy a bond for a new baby for less than $200 and cash it in for $1,000 when he or she is 18 or 19 years old. The $800 gain is the accumulated interest on your $200 investment.

You can purchase zero-coupon Treasury bonds that will mature whenever you want, from next year to 30-years in the future.

So you can select bonds that will come due as your child reaches certain ages. Some can mature at age 18, others at ages 19, 20, 21, and so on. The longer you plan on waiting before collecting the $1,000, the less you pay for each bond.

And the higher interest rates are, the lower the price of each bond will be when you buy it.

What is most important, though, is that it is entirely possible to have your shoe-box money purchase one or more zero-coupon Treasury bonds each year--at least until your child is nine or ten years old. After that, there will be fewer years between his or her age and the time you will most likely want to cash-in their bonds. And the shorter the time such bonds are held, the less they can appreciate.

Even so, for less than $500, you can buy bonds that will be worth $1,000 in eight or nine years. In other words, zero-coupon bonds purchased when your child is ten will still double in value by the time he or she is 18 or 19 (if such bonds pay eight or nine percent interest).

While your child is between one and six years old, you can buy bonds that have at least 18 years to maturity. That means you can purchase bonds for less than $200 when he or she is one, that will be worth $1,000 at age 19. Those bought for $200 when he or she is two will be worth $1,000 at age 20, and so on.

And as long as you purchase only U.S. Treasury bonds, there is absolutely no risk of default. You do, of course, face a risk if you want to sell your bonds before maturity. If interest rates rise sharply after you buy, and you then try to sell, you will not be able to sell your bonds for what you paid for them.

But if you know you are going to hold each bond until maturity, there is no reason to worry about its fluctuating market value. No matter what happens to interest rates after you buy, you will receive $1,000 for each bond held until maturity.

The one negative factor with zero-coupon bonds is their tax status.

Although these bonds do not pay annual dividends or interest, you, or your children, are responsible for the taxes on the "phantom" interest--the annual appreciation of the bond's value.

Some people, because of the annual tax liability on such bonds, would rather invest in anything *but* zero-coupon bonds.

My view is that you have to pay taxes on any taxable investment. In some cases, the taxes can be deferred until the asset is sold, which is the case with stocks.

But if it is a taxable investment, someone will pay the taxes sometime--either year-by-year or in the future.

By paying the taxes on your zero-coupon bonds as you go along, at least the total value of the asset ($1,000) is yours at maturity.

And there can be a tax advantage if the bonds are held in your child's name. If your child is under age 14, there is the $500 annual exemption for unearned income (and the next $500 is taxed at the child's rate). Therefore, if you have less than $12,000 invested in zero-coupon bonds, the interest will be close to tax free. If you invest more than $12,000 in zero-coupon bonds while your child is under age 14, the interest above $1,000 will be taxed at your rate. (I do not mean $12,000 in maturity value, which would be 12 bonds. I mean $12,000 invested in such bonds, which would be approximately 60 bonds, with a maturity value of $60,000.)

If your child is 14 or older, the accumulating interest in zero-coupon bonds will be taxed at his or her lower rate.

And because the annual interest grows as the bonds appreciate in value, the greatest annual appreciation and, therefore, the greatest taxable interest, can take place when your child is 14 or older.

Tax-free zero-coupon bonds do exist. They are issued by municipalities. But they are not risk free. And, as a general rule, unless you are in the highest tax bracket, you are better off with a taxable return and paying your taxes. That is because market pressures normally generate a yield on tax-free bonds that is close to break-even for those with high incomes. As a result, for most of us, tax-free returns are usually less than taxable interest minus the taxes.

The big advantages of zero-coupon Treasury bonds are that they can be purchased for low prices (less than $200 if bought for a new child to come due when he or she is 20 or 21 years old), they lock in a compound rate of return, you know exactly what they will be worth at maturity, and you know you will get your money.

The main disadvantage is the annual tax that must be paid on the "calculated," but unpaid, interest. Although the money to pay the annual taxes must be taken from somewhere else--another investment or other income--I believe that the end result is more than worth the trouble.

You can buy zero-coupon Treasury bonds at any brokerage firm and through custodial accounts at your bank or brokerage firm.

But remember:

* You do not want to buy zero-coupon bonds or any other long-term, interest-bearing investment if you expect interest rates to rise. It is better to keep your funds invested in short-term, interest-bearing accounts until rates increase. Then lock in the higher rates for the long run.

* If interest rates rise unexpectedly after you buy zero-coupon bonds, it is not the end of the world. It means that you missed a chance to do better. But that is not the worst thing that can happen.

* The one true problem with rising interest rates is that they lower the market value of your bond. Therefore, you want to buy zero-coupon bonds with maturity dates that correspond to the times you want to cash them in. That way, you can avoid the problem of having to sell at a loss if interest rates increase after you buy.

Summary

Zero-coupon Treasury bonds are an excellent choice for a child's portfolio. They let you lock in compound interest for many years. There is no risk of default. You know exactly how much each bond will be worth at maturity--$1,000. You can choose bonds with maturity dates that correspond to when you expect to spend the money. And you can purchase zero-coupon bonds for relatively low prices--somewhere around $200 each.

The one disadvantage is that taxes are due each year on the "calculated" but unpaid interest.

Even so, there is a tax break on the first $1,000 of unearned income for a child under 14. And for children 14 or older, the accumulating interest is taxed at their lower rate.

At the very worst, if your child is younger than 14, you will pay taxes at your rate on annual interest above $1,000. In return, you get to earn compound interest at a locked-in rate--an incredible advantage if you buy zero-coupon Treasury bonds when interest rates are relatively high (over eight percent).

Series EE Savings Bonds

At one time, Series EE savings bonds were one of the worst investments you could make. But no longer.

Series EE bonds issued after December 31, 1989 have three outstanding advantages.

One is that they pay an adjustable rate of interest. If you hold your bonds for at least five years, the return is calculated to be equal to "85 percent of the average market yield on five-year Treasury securities during the holding period, compounded semi-annually." That is a great advantage. It means you do not have to worry about inflation or about what might happen to market interest rates. As long as you are earning an adjustable rate of interest, you will do OK. Your returns will adjust to meet changing market conditions.

The second advantage of Series EE bonds is that taxes are not due until the bonds are cashed. That may not seem important, but it is. The after-tax return on any interest-bearing investment is always greater if the taxes are due at the end of the holding period rather than paid on each year's interest. That is because all your money is invested and reinvested (the power of compound interest) until maturity. If you have to pay taxes on each year's interest, then only a fraction of each year's return is reinvested for the next year.

In fact, if you pay taxes on the accumulated interest on Series EE bonds, the after-tax return will be almost equal to the return on five-year Treasury securities, even though the Series EE bonds pay only 85 percent of the average five-year rate. And if the Series EE interest is tax free, you will come out way ahead.

The third advantage of Series EE savings bonds is that they offer one of the few remaining tax breaks. If you buy Series EE Treasury bonds and use the proceeds for higher education expenses (tuition and books), all the interest is tax free.

You can use the money for your education, your spouse's education, or your child's education.

However, if the money is to be used for your child's education, to qualify for tax-free status, the bonds cannot be in your child's name. They must be in the name of either one or both parents. But that's good. It means you can invest money for your child's future education without giving up control of the funds. It also means there is no gift tax to worry about.

On the surface, Series EE bonds do not appear to pay the highest return. But because taxes are not paid until the bonds are sold, they actually pay a real rate of return that can be as high as that of taxable bonds. The return is definitely equal to that of tax-free municipal bonds. And with Series EE bonds, there is absolutely no risk of default.

Plus, they can be purchased for as little as $25 each, with no fees or commissions.

Series EE bonds (sometimes called "education" bonds) are a type of zero-coupon bond. You buy them at a deep discount and wait until maturity to collect all your interest. Instead of annual interest payments, your earnings continue to accumulate at a compound rate over time.

But Series EE bonds have two advantages over other zero-coupon bonds. One is that the earnings can be tax free. The other is that there are no annual tax obligations for the "phantom" interest accumulation. Taxes--if any --are paid only when the bonds are cashed. And at the current "guaranteed" rate, Series EE savings bonds will double in value in about ten years.

A third advantage is that Series EE bonds pay a variable rate of interest if they are held at least five years. That can be a big plus if you want to purchase bonds when market interest rates are relatively low, or if interest rates rise after you buy. On the other hand, if market interest rates are high, there is an advantage to locking in those high rates with a normal zero-coupon bond.

So far, so good for Series EE savings bonds. In fact, a tax-free, risk-free, market-based rate of return is a great opportunity. And because Series EE bonds can be held for up to 30 years before they stop earning interest, you can buy them from the time your child is born up to five years before his or her estimated last year of college.

Even if your child decides not to go to college, the worst that can happen is that you have to pay taxes on the interest. But a tax-deferred, market-based rate of return that is equal to 85 percent of the yield on five-year Treasury securities is a good deal. Even if you have to pay taxes on your returns, you will end up about the same as if you had invested in a bond with a higher, but annually-taxable, rate of return.

For example, a $1,000 investment that pays eight percent annual interest and is taxed at 28 percent will be worth $1,750 in ten years.

A series EE bond that earns 85 percent of that eight percent, but is not taxed until it is cashed, will be worth $1,670 in ten years--after paying a 28 percent tax on the $931 gain.

There is a small difference between these two alternatives. But the Series EE bond holds its own, even if the interest is taxed.

If there were no drawbacks, Series EE bonds would be an unqualified recommendation. Every time you had $25 or $50 in your shoe box, you could stop at a bank or S&L and buy another Series EE bond.

Whether you buy bonds for $25 or $1,000, the return is exactly the same. And because there are no fees for buying and selling, Series EE bonds are one of the few investments that do not discriminate against small purchases.

Unfortunately, there is one possible drawback.

There is a "catch" to the tax-free offer. The tax-free status is a function of your income. Currently, the entire interest is tax-free only if your adjusted gross income is less than $60,000 in the year the bonds are cashed. There is a sliding scale of taxes that applies to the interest as your adjusted gross income exceeds $60,000.

The IRS will adjust the $60,000 figure to keep up with inflation. But you are betting that your income in 15- to 20-years will be the equivalent of $60,000 today.

Even so, because of their tax-deferred status, these bonds are a good investment even if you do have to pay taxes on the earned interest.

In effect, Series EE savings bonds are a "win" or "win more" opportunity. If you qualify for the tax-free interest, they are an excellent investment. If you end up paying taxes on the interest, they are still the equal of other bonds.

Series EE bonds are one of the only investments that defer taxes while, at the same time, being risk free.

And because of their variable rate of return, Series EE bonds may be one of the best choices of all.

One small concern is that these "education" bonds are new. They began in 1990. So it will be years before the first ones are cashed in and used for education expenses. Although these bonds have a lot to offer, they are also an unknown.

But if you do not think the $60,000 adjusted gross income limit will be a problem, and if you are pretty certain your children will go to college, Series EE bonds are a great place to put some money.

As of now, you can buy them at commercial banks, savings institutions, or through many Payroll Savings Plans for as little as $25. And there are no fees or commissions!

But the tax-free interest applies only to bonds issued after December 31, 1989. And there is one strange restriction. The person buying a bond that will qualify for tax-free status must be at least 24 years old.

Also, you should be careful to keep records of all such bonds. Otherwise, you may run into a lot of red tape when you want to claim the tax exclusion.

Your local IRS office will tell you what records to keep. (Essentially, you use IRS form 8818 to record each bond's serial number, issue date, and face value when cashed. Later you will need receipts from an educational institution.)

There is one other sensible use for Series EE bonds.

They can be purchased in your child's name and kept in your child's account. You or your spouse can be listed as a beneficiary--not co-owner. And the interest will accumulate tax-deferred.

When your child cashes in the bonds, the accumulated interest will be taxed at his or her rate, rather than yours.

But remember, if you choose to put Series EE bonds in your child's name, the interest will not be tax free, even if it is used for education.

Here are a few other notes on Series EE savings bonds.

* No more than $15,000 can be invested in Series EE bonds in any one calendar year by any one person.

* Savings bonds are not marketable. They can be cashed in after six months. But they cannot be sold to another person.

* There is a minimum guaranteed interest for bonds held at least five years. You will receive either six percent (the current guarantee) or 85 percent of the average yield on five-year Treasury securities, whichever is larger.

* Series EE savings bonds are always exempt from state and local income taxes.

Summary

Series EE savings bonds are an excellent way to invest for your child's future.

If held for at least five years, Series EE bonds pay either a guaranteed minimum return (currently six percent compound interest) or a variable rate (85 percent of the average yield on five-year Treasury securities), whichever is higher.

In either case, the interest is compounded. There is no risk of default. The bonds can be cashed after six months. They earn interest for 30 years. They cannot fall in value. They can only appreciate. They can be purchased for as little as $25. There are no fees or commissions to buy or sell. They can be bought and sold at banks or savings institutions. And because taxes are deferred until they are cashed, the actual yield is comparable to higher yields on bonds that pay semi-annual dividends that are taxed yearly.

Plus, if the money is used for education (tuition and books) for you, your spouse, or your child, and if you meet the income limitations, all the interest is tax free. And the money is not transferred to your child's control.

Of course, it can also be smart to buy Series EE bonds in your child's name. If you do, the interest will not be tax free, even if it is used for education. But the investment will grow at a compound rate. And taxes can be deferred until your child is 14 or older.

Custodial Accounts (Uniform Gift to Minors Act or Uniform Transfers to Minors Act)

The third part of our basic investment plan is a custodial account--sometimes called a Uniform Gift to Minor's or Uniform Transfers to Minor's account, after the Acts that established the current tax rules.

This is the account that lets you invest money in your child's name.

You can open such an account at almost any bank, brokerage firm, or mutual fund.

But all accounts are not the same.

So check the differences before you make a decision. What you want to ask is:

What is the minimum opening balance?

It should be whatever you choose to deposit. If someone wants a relatively large initial deposit or requires large additions to the account, you should go somewhere else--unless they have something special to offer to make up for the inconvenience.

What happens to each deposit?

All the money in such an account should be immediately invested in CDs or at money-market interest rates. If you are told that the money will earn a passbook savings rate unless you accumulate enough to purchase a CD, talk to someone else. There is absolutely no reason to give up two to four percent on money left in such an account.

What investments can be made within the account?

You should be able to purchase Treasury bonds, at the very least. And you might want the chance to buy stocks. If your only option is a CD (which is the case at some commercial banks), you will not be able to do much.

Are there any fees?

You should be able to open such an account without having to pay either an initiation fee or an annual fee.

How large are the commissions to buy stocks and bonds?

This is a tricky issue. You might have to accept somewhat higher commissions in return for more investment choices.

But remember: If you end up with an account you do not like, you can always change later. You are not locked in to your choice for life. You can switch whenever you want. It is your child's account. And it is under your control.

So if something doesn't seem right, ask about it. Maybe it can be fixed. If not, take your business somewhere else.

Summary

Custodial accounts are, or should be, a no-fee, no-charge place to make investments in your child's name. All deposits--no matter how small--should earn money-market interest rates.

And with most such accounts, you can buy and sell stocks and bonds without withdrawing your funds. You simply call and make a switch. Of course, you have to pay commissions when you buy and sell. So you should shop around a bit to compare commissions at different places. But when you do, do not forget that the accounts with the highest commissions may offer other advantages or services in return. So do not choose the account with the lowest commission without understanding what you might be giving up.

A fourth basic part of our plan is a "cash management account," either in your name or, preferably, held jointly with your spouse.

There is not much to say about these accounts. But they are available at any brokerage firm and many banks. They pay competitive short-term rates on all deposits. Funds can be switched into stocks, bonds, and precious metals with a phone call. And it can make sense to have a separate account to make investments for your child that will be kept in your name until you decide to transfer them to your child.

Investment du Jour

Garrison Keillor's "mythical little town that time forgot"--Lake Wobegon--has a cafe. And the cafe's menu features "hotdish du jour."

If you grew up in the midwest, surrounded by hotdishes at every gathering, the idea of a menu with "hotdish du jour" is pretty funny.

But when it comes to investing, especially for our children, it is not funny to see people getting caught up in fads, or ordering the "investment of the day."

One of the main purposes of this book is to help you establish a simple, workable, profitable saving and investment plan for your children. I cannot say that sensible new ideas will not come along. I can say that if you have a solid plan in place and a good understanding of a few basic investments, there is not much chance you will be taken in by the hype that surrounds each new pie-in-the-sky idea.

That is because you will have a benchmark. You will be able to compare whatever new idea is being sold to something real. And if you can do that, you can decide for yourself what is and is not sensible.

Those who are most likely to fall for a "too good to be true" scheme are those who are doing nothing. They are the ones who are looking for the one big score to bail them out.

But if you have a plan in place, the only ideas that will make sense are those that can do better than what you are already doing.

Of course, most "new ideas" are not really new. Sometimes truly new opportunities do occur, opportunities that did not exist in the past. But most of the time, what you will see is someone "rediscovering" the "incredible benefits" of an investment idea that has been around for many years.

Therefore, I want to give you a little information on a few of the most common investments.

I will try to be as straightforward as I can. But there is no way to hide my opinion of each investment's place in a child's portfolio.

More importantly, I do not want to give you a negative impression of any legitimate investment. My major concern with many popular investments is that they require lot of knowledge and a real time commitment if you are going to be successful. Almost any legitimate investment can make sense for an adult portfolio, if you are willing and able to put in the time to learn about it and to follow it on a daily basis.

But few of us have the time to become "experts" on investments just so we can include them in a child's portfolio.

Common stocks

The two standard arguments for including common stocks in a child's portfolio are:

1) Common stocks have unlimited potential. Unlike interest-bearing securities, with stocks, the sky is the limit.

2) Taxes on your profits are not due until the stock is sold. Therefore, stocks can be sold when your child is age 14 or older, which means that all the profits can be taxed at the child's lower rate.

Those are great arguments.

Unfortunately, they only make sense if the stocks you buy appreciate in value. And even non-experts know there are no guarantees in the stock market.

If a stock analyst could unfailingly pick stocks that would double in value every eight to ten years, he or she would be one of the most famous stock-pickers of all time. But that is exactly what you can do with zero-coupon Treasury bonds or Series EE savings bonds. And with those government bonds, there is absolutely no chance you will pick a loser.

No one has ever been able to select only winning stocks. No one ever will. And the great error that is made when considering stocks as a primary investment for a child's portfolio is to get caught up in greed--to look at the big winners and ignore the big losers.

But I cannot tell everyone to avoid stocks.

If you are a successful stock-market investor, you will not want to pass up a chance to do the best you can for your children. But if you are not an experienced, and successful, stock-market investor, the fact that you are investing for your children will not guarantee success.

It is possible to prepare a scenario that makes any investment market look like a fantastic opportunity. All you have to do is pick the right time period to cover, or concentrate on the winners while ignoring the losers.

Picking the "right" stock is a great experience. Not only do you make a bundle of money. You also get a big boost to your ego. If you pick a winning stock, you feel as though you outsmarted everyone else, or at least beat the market.

But that is the tip-off to the dangers in stocks. Anytime you feel that you have to "beat the market" in order to make a profitable investment, you are admitting that the market is working against you. At the very least, you understand that the market is "not your friend."

I am sure that anyone who has ever looked at the stock market remembers a stock they should have bought--a stock that went through the roof. But most of us forget about all the stocks we thought about that went nowhere but down.

The one rule of thumb for investing in stocks--and every broker will (or should) tell it to you is: "Only invest money you can afford to lose." For most of us, the money in our children's portfolios is not money we can afford to lose.

Mutual funds

Mutual funds collect money from many individual investors and then use that money to buy a large number of different securities. The idea behind a mutual fund is that by purchasing a wide variety of securities, the risk of loss is reduced. That is true. But the opportunity for large gains is also eliminated. That is why mutual funds seldom have promotions based on big winnings.

Instead, mutual funds advertise their past achievements in one of two ways: How well they did compared to the market, or how well they did compared to similar mutual funds.

Unfortunately, neither measurement is a guarantee for the future. A mutual fund that returned a good profit last year may have done so by choosing stocks that others passed up. But in a cyclical world, the stocks that were last year's big winners can easily be this year's or next year's big losers.

Even so, for most families, mutual funds are a better choice than individual stocks.

But if you follow the world of mutual funds, you will see that the big goal is, once again, to "beat the market."

In other words, the managers and researchers for mutual funds are trying to do exactly what each of us would like to do--win a game that is stacked against them. How successful are they? That is not always easy to see.

The typical mutual fund tends to do a little better than the stock market (as measured by an index such as the Dow Jones Industrial Average) when the market is rising. But mutual funds can do worse than the market when the market is falling. Therefore, if the stock market were some sort of "perfect" cycle, the gains would be washed out by the losses. But over time the stock market tends to cycle higher. As a result, mutual funds tend to gain value over time, as well.

However, there is a big difference between saying there is a positive gain over time and that there will be a positive gain during the time you own a particular mutual fund. Mutual funds did pretty well from 1982 until mid-1987. But the stock market crashed in 1987. And so did the values of mutual funds.

If you invest in mutual funds for your children, chances are the investment will be held long enough to gain from the upward drift of the stock market. But if you were someone who had planned on using your mutual fund investments in 1988 or 1989, you would have been in for an unpleasant surprise. Of course, if you held on after the crash of 1987, by 1990, you would have been ahead again.

But I do not think it is reasonable to expect the stock market of the 1990s to equal the performance of the 1980s. And I caution you to put the "track records" that indicate past performance in perspective before deciding that mutual funds are a good choice.

You should also be aware of the fact that there are many different kinds of mutual funds. So far, I have been referring to mutual funds that invest in a broad range of stocks. But many funds invest in specialized stocks. Some invest primarily in "growth" stocks-- stocks that are expected to gain in value rather than yield high dividends. Others select only foreign stocks, precious metals stocks, income stocks (dividends instead of growth), and so on. Some invest in bonds or short term securities. Some choose combinations.

There are so many mutual funds that no matter which market category you pick, you can find a mutual fund that specializes in that area.

Some funds charge relatively high fees--both to buy and sell, as well as to cover annual management costs. Others have no fees for buying and selling. But almost all have a built-in annual charge. And the charges can be high enough to wipe out a considerable part of your gains. So check carefully before you act.

If you are on any investment mailing lists, you have probably received advertisements from "experts" who claim they can (for a fee) help you earn a good return by telling you when to switch from one type of mutual fund to another. That is not a totally false claim. As economic conditions change, certain stocks will do better than others. But trying to beat the market by switching back and forth is a tough path to follow over the years.

If you believe that the stock market offers potential returns that outweigh the returns on interest-bearing securities, then I suggest you follow the old standby investment plan. Invest a given amount of money each month or every two or three months (but stick to your schedule) in a mutual fund that matches the market. Instead of trying to beat the market, just go along with it. And do not sell until some time in the future.

If you follow such a plan, you will buy more stocks when stock prices are low and less when stock prices are high. You will not lose by trying to guess the tops and bottoms of cycles. And you will accumulate value that matches the market itself.

Over time, your investment should return a good profit.

But it will not be a lot higher than what you could earn if you invest in government securities--especially if you buy zero-coupon bonds when interest rates are high.

And it could be lower, because there is absolutely no guarantee in the stock market.

Is it "fair" to keep saying that there are no guarantees in stocks? I think it is.

In the first place, there are some guarantees when you invest in government securities.

In the second place, when you are investing for your child's future, you should look for all the guarantees you can get.

Regular government bonds

The standard government bond pays semi-annual dividends. Instead of automatically reinvesting the interest on your initial investment, the interest is given to you twice a year. And you have to figure out what to do with it.

As a rule, the time to buy bonds of any kind is when interest rates are relatively high. If rates are expected to rise in the future, you should wait before making a long-term commitment.

Keep your money earning short-term interest until long-term rates are high enough to justify locking up your money. And remember--it is locking up your money. Because if interest rates increase after you buy a bond, you are stuck with it, unless you are willing to sell at a loss.

But no matter how high long-term interest rates go, your return on normal bonds is not compounded. How much difference does compound interest make? A lot.

Here is an example that does not really apply to a child's account. But it is interesting anyway.

When George Washington and his troops were huddled at Valley Forge, they had run out of supplies and money. Washington wrote to a wealthy citizen, who lived nearby, and explained that unless funds could be raised, the army would have to be disbanded. This citizen apparently gave Washington $450,000 in cash and supplies. It was all he had. But it was enough to keep the army together. And to give us the chance to win our independence.

But the loan was never repaid. And the descendants of the lender, who died penniless, sued the government for the money it owed them. Using a six percent rate of interest, which was the rate at the time of the Revolutionary War, by 1990 the value of the loan was more than $140 billion--if it were compounded daily. If it were compounded annually, it was worth $90 billion.

That is a lot of money. And a big difference.

So if you choose to invest in bonds that pay semi-annual dividends, you should have a good idea of what you will do with all the interest you receive. As I mentioned earlier, one option is to invest the interest in Series EE savings bonds.

Precious metals

If you are scared to death of inflation, you will probably end up buying some tangible assets. Precious metals, and gold and silver coins, are marketed heavily in this country. And anyone who is afraid of inflation is going to listen to the sales pitch:

* People from around the world have chosen to put funds into precious metals for many years.

* Gold and silver have helped many people through times of economic disaster and political upheaval.

* And precious metals have appreciated faster than the rate of inflation.

It is a pretty good sales pitch. But the argument is not really applicable to America.

America is not in danger of either political or economic collapse. Nor is America in danger of falling victim to a hyperinflation.

On the other hand, it looks as though we may be stuck with a four to five percent average rate of inflation for many years to come. And a four to five percent rate of inflation is enough to distort the markets and to affect the returns on every investment.

Therefore, I can understand the appeal of tangible assets.

But it is important to understand the complexities in the tangible assets markets before investing any money.

There are two broad categories of tangible assets: those bought as collectibles (hopefully by people who appreciate them for what they are, rather than by someone who hopes to make a quick buck) and those bought as strict investments.

Truly rare coins fit into the first category. Gold and silver bullion belong in the second. Then there are the overlaps--gold and silver coins, for example, that are not truly "rare," but are scarce enough to command prices above their bullion content.

Although the highest prices obviously go to the true collectibles, the average investor has no business buying collectibles as an investment. The true collector may make a large profit on his or her collection. But it was a collection bought with knowledge and interest. The profit, if any, is an extra.

Unfortunately, there are many national telemarketers selling "collectibles" as investments. And it is difficult to dismiss the appeal of million-dollar coins. But I recommend that you keep your greed in check and stay away from such sales pitches.

If you do not have the required knowledge, you will not know what you are buying. And all collectibles are not equal when it comes to future potential. Also, there are large markups on many collectibles, both when you buy and when you sell. It is not uncommon to pay a 20 percent markup over wholesale when you buy and receive a 20 percent markdown from retail when you sell. Viewed as a retail business, such profit margins may not seem out of line.

But as investments, such collectibles are questionable. As a rule of thumb, the retail prices of such collectibles have to double for you to break even after paying your buy and sell "commissions."

An equally significant problem is that few of us can judge the quality of high-priced collectibles. And with rare coins, for example, a slightly higher quality can cause the price to double or triple. That is not a problem for an expert who can tell the difference. But if you are not an expert, you may overpay. And if you do, you may never get your original investment back.

So if you want to add some tangible assets to your child's portfolio, I recommend you stay with bullion or gold and silver coins that are priced according to their bullion content.

I prefer gold to either silver or platinum because gold is mainly an investment metal. Silver and platinum are used as industrial metals and their prices are affected by many unforseen economic circumstances.

Gold is the most international precious metal. And it can be purchased in small bars or in newly-minted coins that are not intended for circulation (not "real" money).

The larger the size of the bar or coin, the lower the premium. But all gold investments carry some premium over the "spot price" that is reported in the daily paper. The spot price is really a wholesale price.

And although you can calculate the markup over the spot price on a one-ounce bar and a ten-ounce bar, the difference is not of much significance. It stays the same when you buy and sell. What does matter is the price difference between dealers. And that can vary by a wide margin. So if you want to buy gold, get prices from a number of reputable dealers before you buy.

But remember, as the "premium" increases--meaning that the markup over the spot price of gold gets larger--you are either getting into collectibles, which you want to avoid unless you have help from an expert you can trust, or you may be getting a bad deal.

I have to tell you that it makes me nervous to discuss precious metals at all. Not because they are a terrible idea. But because I do not believe the average person should put a large percentage of a child's portfolio into precious metals. And because I know that if you buy any precious metals or coins at all, you are likely to run into a high-pressure sales pitch to buy more. And the salesman can be convincing, especially if you are legitimately worried about the consequences of inflation.

On the other hand, if you want to become an expert on precious metals or collectibles, such as rare coins, there are many books available. But you should read more than one book before making major decisions. Many books are written by dealers and do not give you an unbiased view of the subject.

These are interesting markets. But they take time to learn. And unless you are already an expert, you should put only a small percentage of your child's money into such investments.

Annuities

Annuities are normally sold as a retirement investment—a vehicle that earns interest while deferring taxes. But with so many older parents of young children (me, for one), annuities are also being marketed as an investment possibility for our children.

Essentially, annuities are simple.

You buy one, normally for $1,000 to $10,000, and earn interest that is not paid and not taxed until sometime in the future.

Because taxes are deferred, annuities are often called "tax shelters." But I think that is being a little hopeful. It is one thing to discuss the possibility of deferring taxes. It is another to claim that doing so will result in lower taxes.

For some reason, it is commonly assumed that if you put off taxes on some income until you are retired that you will definitely pay a lower tax rate on that income. Sometimes that is true. Sometimes it is not. Many retired people have incomes that are higher than they had while they were working, because of pensions and investments. They can, therefore, end up paying higher, not lower, taxes. Also, no one knows what the tax rates will be in 20 or 30 years. So how can anyone be certain that it is a good idea to pay taxes later, rather than now?

But there are other, more serious, problems with annuities.

1) Annuities are not risk free. They are issued by private corporations--insurance companies. Therefore, there is a risk of default. To remove that risk, many annuities are now insured. But, as in any market, less risk means a lower return.

2) If you withdraw any money from an annuity before age 59 1/2, it is taxed fully. Plus, you have to pay a ten percent penalty tax on the earnings withdrawn. Therefore, if you are planning on using the earnings from an annuity for your child, be sure you will be 59 1/2 when you want to spend the money.

3) Annuities pay a return set by the insurance company. The first year's yield is always fairly high. After that, you have no idea of what you will earn.

4) To "protect" you against low returns in the future, annuities offer a "guarantee." But it is a slippery guarantee. All it does is give you the right to withdraw your funds without a penalty if the return slips below a guaranteed level. That is important because the insurance company has the right to penalize you by as much as 25 percent for early withdrawals, meaning that the insurance company can legally keep a large chunk of your money. Unfortunately, the guaranteed return is very low. In 1990, it was around four to four-and-a-half percent. In other words, you could get stuck with a very low return--five percent or so--and not be able to do anything with your money without giving a large portion of it to the insurer who issued the annuity.

Plus, if you buy an annuity instead of a zero-coupon Treasury bond when interest rates are high, you miss the chance to secure that high return for many years into the future. Your returns are locked in until maturity with zero-coupon bonds. The returns on annuities can fall to very low levels in the years ahead.

5) The interest you receive from annuities is dependent on the size of your investment. The $1,000 annuities pay the lowest rates. The yields on a $10,000 annuity are higher.

6) When the money is received, after you reach age 59 1/2, you still pay taxes on it at your tax rate. So I am not sure why annuities can be called "tax shelters."

Obviously, annuities are not my favorite investment.

But before anyone asks, "Where else can you get a low risk, tax deferred investment?" let me say that Series EE savings bonds offer everything annuities can give you--and more.

Series EE savings bonds are risk free. They have no penalty for early withdrawal, although your actual return will be higher if you hold your bonds for at least five years. The variable interest rate paid on Series EE bonds will almost certainly be higher than the returns on annuities. The guaranteed minimum interest is definitely higher. Series EE bonds defer income and taxes, just as annuities do. You can buy Series EE bonds for as little as $25. And Series EE bonds do not discriminate against small investments--they all earn the same return.

As a straight investment, Series EE savings bonds beat annuities at every turn. Plus, if the Series EE bonds are used for education, making all the interest tax free, there is no contest at all.

Whether or not you use the tax-free advantage of Series EE savings bonds, they offer an excellent way to accumulate wealth for your child.

Summary of our "investments du jour"

- Individual stocks are a relatively risky choice for a child's portfolio. But if you believe that you know enough to beat the odds, you should consider buying stocks in your name. Later, you can transfer only the winners to your child's account before selling them. That way the profits will be taxed at your child's lower rate. And by keeping the losers in your name, you can use them as a tax deduction for yourself.
- Mutual funds are probably the "safest" of the investments discussed in this chapter. But the risks are very real. And no matter how attractive the sales literature is, it is tough to argue that the "chance" of earning a little more than the yields on Treasury bonds is worth the risk.

   One advantage, however, is that you can open an account at many mutual funds for as little as $250 and make additional investments of only $25.

   And if you want to take the time to learn how to manage such an account, you can switch your investment from one type of fund to another with a phone call--from a growth fund, for example, to a bond fund, and then to a foreign stock fund, and so on.

- Annuities, which only make sense if you or your spouse will be at least 59-1/2 years old when your child needs the earnings, have nothing to offer that is not achieved better with Series EE savings bonds. The only problem with Series EE savings bonds is that they sound dull.
- Bonds that pay semi-annual dividends are not terrible. But they do not pay compound interest over time. Therefore, if you want to lock in high interest rates, zero-coupon Treasury bonds are a better choice. Plus, you can buy zero-coupon bonds for around $200. Regular bonds sell for about $1,000 each.

  If you do decide to invest in regular bonds, be sure you know what you will do with the semi-annual interest payments. One possibility is to invest the interest in Series EE savings bonds. Another is to use some of it to pay taxes on appreciating zero-coupon bonds.

- Precious metals should be treated with caution. They do not pay interest. Prices can vary from dealer to dealer. And although they are viewed as protection against inflation, prices can stagnate or fall for years unless inflation soars to frightening levels. As a rule, these investments are better left to professionals. Also, after the inflation of the 1970s, it is virtually certain that market pressures will keep interest rates high enough to account for inflation, something that was not true in the 1960s and 1970s. Therefore, precious metals are no longer the only way to stay ahead of inflation.

Miscellaneous Ideas

T his chapter is very personal--to me and, I expect, to you as well.

It is personal because it looks at real life--at the "non-financial" parts of child finance. It is about toys and antiques and the collections we loved as children.

I cannot possibly include every idea that could be a part of this chapter. I cannot even do justice to the few I will discuss.

But I could not write a book about saving and investing for children without including some thoughts on the things that touch our lives as children.

Antiques

When I was teaching economics in the SUNY system (in the mid-1970s), I spent time looking for antique furniture. Not expensive antiques. Just nice old furniture.

I met an antique dealer who told me how he got started in the business.

When he was first married, he and his wife went out and bought a house full of new furniture. One year later, they had to move. And to make it as much fun as possible, they decided to sell everything and start fresh. They sold their furniture for 40- to 50-cents on the dollar, losing more than half the money they had spent just one year earlier.

He swore that he would never again buy a piece of new furniture. Little by little, they moved from used to old to antique. And one day he realized that they had collected so much stuff that he decided to open an antique store.

I never bought anything from him. But I did slowly accumulate a number of things that I liked. None were bought as investments. All were bought because I liked them. I still own some--a pine blanket chest I bought at an auction in Vermont that is in my youngest daughter's room, some old pine chairs, and a pine table.

I also sold some things over the years. And I made a "profit" on each one.

My intention was not to make a profit. It was to buy what I liked, hoping that I would always be able to sell it for what I paid for it. Fortunately, what I liked was older furniture that appreciated, rather than depreciated, in value over the years.

You can do the same when furnishing your child's room--if you like antiques.

With a little time spent poking around antique stores, even household sales, you can find cribs, chests, rocking chairs, even quilts, that will hold their value. If you keep them long enough, they should gain in value.

You are not going to make a lot of money. But it can be fun. And if you keep the furniture, your child will almost certainly be able to sell it for a good price when he or she is an adult.

Baseball cards

When I was eleven years old (in 1952) I collected baseball cards. I had a great time putting together a complete set of what is now a very valuable collector's item.

Of course, the cards were not worth anything in 1952. But I packed them away in a box, anyway, and put them in the attic.

In the late 1970s, maybe 25 years later, I found out that my long-forgotten baseball cards were worth more than $1,000. So when I went home to visit my parents the next summer, I dug around the attic looking for my "investment." But I could not find my cards. And my parents had no idea of what had happened to them.

Each year, the price of my old set went up. And each summer that I returned home, I dug through the attic again.

By 1990, the set was worth as much as $40,000. But it is still lost. My only consolation is that I probably would have sold the set for $1,000 if I had found it that first summer. My hope is that someday in the future, when the price is even higher, I will discover my lost treasure.

Today, collecting baseball cards can be serious business. Many investors buy cards by the case and store the cases unopened. Each case contains 20 boxes of cards. But no one knows which cards. The contents of each case is a mystery.

No one knows exactly what is in each case. Because the cases are not opened. They are bought and sold according to the original year of issue. And their market value is a function of their "rookie cards"--how many rookies in a particular year went on to become stars! The more there were, the more that year's case is worth.

For example, in 1986, you could have bought a new case of baseball cards for about $230. By mid-1990, that case was worth from $5,300 to $6,000, because there were a number of "stars" who began playing in the major leagues in 1986.

Whether or not the adult business of investing in baseball cards you never see sounds like fun, it has been a profitable venture. As far as I know, every case of cards has appreciated from its original price.

But there are even more investors and collectors who buy and sell individual cards or complete sets (52 cards).

For our purposes, however, the lesson is to take care of your child's collections. Aside from their sentimental value, they could be worth the down payment on a house or a large chunk of college costs.

Toys

Toys, unlike baseball cards or other kids' collectibles, are usually bought by parents, grandparents, or family friends.

But wherever they come from, do not throw them away!

The demand for old toys has sent prices soaring. And "old" does not mean what "old" used to mean.

The toys of our youth are already valuable collectibles.

It used to be said that something had to be 100 years old before it could be called an antique. That may still be true. But antique or not, toys that are less than 30 years old are worth hundreds, sometimes thousands, of dollars.

Electric trains, Barbie dolls, comic books, whatever. They are worth incredible sums today.

Which of today's toys will be worth the most in the future? There is no way of knowing for certain. So keep everything.

Art

In 1990, a Japanese businessman purchased a painting by Renoir for $82.5 million.

That is a little steep for decorating a child's room.

But it is not out of the question to buy real art for your child.

Posters and many original prints can be purchased for about the same price as department store "art." They are more beautiful. I believe they are more stimulating for children. And they might be sold for a profit sometime in the future.

Summary

The recommendation of this chapter is: Do not throw anything away.

But I do not want to turn something wonderful into a mercenary act.

Children's furniture, toys, collectibles, and art should be fun. They should help the child grow and develop. They should be a great pleasure. They should not be bought primarily as an investment.

But that does not mean you cannot have both.

If you are going to buy an electric train, call the local model railroad club. Ask about the best trains to buy. At worst, you will find out which trains are the highest quality. In any case, your child will enjoy having something of quality. And it might be worth a considerable sum of money in the future.

I think that we sometimes forget that children appreciate quality, even that they can tell the difference. But if you think back to when you were a child, you will remember how it felt to have something nice.

There is nothing wrong with putting in a little effort and a little thought when you buy something for your child. Or in taking care of it. And saving it.

The greatest benefit will most likely be the child's appreciation of quality.

On the other hand, at current prices, my old set of baseball cards could now pay for four years of tuition at a public college or university.

A Complete Plan

This is a handbook, not an encyclopedia.

As such, it should do more than simply list all the possibilities.

A handbook should offer guidance, not just information.

If you need bits and pieces of information on all sorts of investment ideas, the bookstores and libraries are full of 600- to 800-page investment "encyclopedias."

The purpose of this book is to fill another need—the need to be able to do something with all that information.

If there is a model for our handbook, it would be a "how to sail" book. There are many books that tell you all sorts of things about all sorts of sailboats. But when it gets down to you and your boat, you need more than an encyclopedia listing all the boats ever made. You need more than an explanation of the advantages and disadvantages of each boat. You need to know more than where to find all the great places in the world to sail. If you want to learn to sail your boat, you need a book that tells you "how to sail!"

And if you want to save and invest for your children's future, this book is an attempt to tell you how to do it.

There is another important similarity between our handbook and a handbook on sailing.

When you sail, you have to work within the constraints of the physical environment.

Financial plans are the same. They always exist within an overall environment that is beyond anyone's control.

A sailor cannot control the weather. And you cannot control the economic, financial, and legal environment you must work with.

Saving and investing for your children can only be done in the environment that exists and within the limitations of your own financial situation.

It might be fun to talk about how things used to be. About what you would do if things were different. About how much money can be made in stocks if you pick the right one at the right time. About what you would do if interest rates went above 20 percent again. About what you would do if inflation soared back into double-digits. Or about how bad the tax laws are.

But if you are on a small boat, caught in a storm, it will not do much good to think about what you would do if you had a bigger boat or a safer boat, or what you would do if there were no storm. If you are going to make it through and enjoy the years ahead, your job is to do the best you can with what you have.

This book offers the best advice I can give you on what to do for your child's financial future.

What you need

Given the overall economic, financial, and tax climate, here is what you need.

1. A shoe box.

2. A Social Security number for your child. You need one by the time he or she is two, anyway.

3. A custodial account so you can make investments in your child's name and take advantage of the tax breaks that do exist.

4. Possibly a trust fund, if you want to put a lot of money in your child's name.

5. A cash management account so you can make investments in your name (or jointly with your spouse) that will later be transferred to your child.

The cost? Nothing.

Unless you want a trust fund, there is no cost to you for setting up any of these other accounts.

Next, you need a few basic investments.

I recommend:

1. Custodial accounts and cash management accounts that earn money market interest on all deposits, no matter how small they are.

2. Zero-coupon Treasury bonds purchased in your child's name. There is the $1,000 tax advantage on unearned income for a child under 14. And for children 14 or older, all income is taxed at their rate, not yours.

3. Series EE savings bonds purchased in your name (or jointly with your spouse). If the money is used for education, all the interest is tax free. If not, you still end up with an excellent investment.

Finally, you want to weigh tax considerations against control.

All money transferred into a custodial account or a trust fund is an irrevocable gift. It is money that, once given, belongs to your child, although he or she cannot take control of the funds until age 18 or 21, depending upon state law.

One important tax consideration is the "Kiddie tax," which says that for a child under age 14, unearned income that exceeds $1,000 per year will be taxed at the parents' highest rate. Therefore, once your child's account is earning more than $1,000 a year in interest, there is no tax advantage in transferring additional funds to the account.

After your child reaches age 14, all income is taxed at the child's rate, which will be lower than your rate. Therefore, there is a tax advantage to earning interest in a child's account rather than in your name if the child is 14 or older.

However, that tax break comes at a cost--the cost of giving up eventual control of the funds. So if you want to put a lot of money in your child's name, whether or not he or she has reached age 14, you must weigh the tax advantages against the loss of control.

One choice that lets you meet both objectives is the Series EE savings bond.

These bonds are purchased in your name, or jointly with your spouse. And when the bonds are cashed, if the money is used for education, all the interest is tax free.

Therefore, you get a tax break, and the funds remain under your control.

If, for whatever reason, the money is not or cannot be used for education (for you, your spouse, or your child), you will have to pay taxes on the interest. But because the interest is allowed to grow at a variable compound rate, free of taxes, you are not going to lose.

In fact, Series EE bonds could turn out to be one of the surprise opportunities in any market.

How much should you put away for your child each month or each year?

That depends on how much you want to have for your child in the future.

The following table makes the calculations easy.

But no matter how easy the calculations are, the stress in today's world makes it difficult to follow through on any financial plan for our children.

You must have an idea of what is necessary to reach a given goal. Otherwise, there is no way of knowing where you will end up in the future. But rigid schedules can become a negative factor.

Here is a common example: You determine what your monthly contributions must be in order to accumulate a given amount of money. Then you begin making the necessary deposits to your child's account. Everything is great, for a while. Then a pressing financial need forces you to miss a few contributions. After a few months have passed, you "owe" your child's account a lot of money--more than you can afford to give in any one month. So you skip a few more months. All of a sudden, it is impossible to catch up. So you abandon your plan and start looking for a "hot deal"-- something that can make a quick bundle. Now you are into risky ventures. And your chance of successfully building a fund for your child has the odds stacked against it.

I have three recommendations, or suggestions.

1) Do not make long-term goal setting your first step. Let your first step be our shoe box. Then get a Social Security number for your child. Then open a custodial account (under the Uniform Gift to Minors Act). Then buy a few zero-coupon Treasury bonds through the custodial account. Then buy some Series EE savings bonds in your name. Then, after a year or so, sit down and see how much you have accomplished.

Very simply, get started before you set any long-term goals.

2) Next, set realistic goals. You can always raise your goals. But if you have to cut back, it can feel like a failure.

3) Finally, if you have to miss a few months, or a year, forget it. As soon as you can, just pick up where you left off. You can try to make up for what you had to skip. But that should not be a major goal. It is much better to have a slightly smaller future portfolio than to abandon your entire plan because of a temporary setback.

Whatever you do is great. So concentrate on doing something instead of on what you might not be able to do because of circumstances you cannot control.

Table

(Explanation begins on the next page)

Child's current age	One-time, single contribution	Equal annual contributions	Equal monthly contributions
1	3.70	36.45	434.67
2	3.42	32.75	389.79
3	3.17	29.33	348.34
4	2.94	26.15	310.07
5	2.72	23.21	274.73
6	2.52	20.50	242.11
7	1.71	17.98	211.98
8	2.16	15.65	184.16
9	2.00	13.49	158.47
10	1.85	11.49	134.76
11	1.71	9.64	112.86
12	1.59	7.92	92.63
13	1.47	6.34	73.96
14	1.36	4.87	56.72
15	1.26	3.51	40.80
16	1.17	2.25	26.10
17	1.08	1.08	12.53

The figures in this table are based on an 8 percent rate of return.

And they can be used in at least two different ways:

- To calculate the future value of single, annual, or monthly contributions.
- To calculate the single, annual, or monthly contributions needed to reach a given future value.

Calculating future portfolio values

- To determine the future value of a single contribution, find the number in the "single-payment" column that corresponds to your child's current age. Then multiply that number by the one-time investment.

  For example, a single $10,000 investment made when your child is four years old will be worth $29,400 when he or she is eighteen ($10,000 times 2.94).

- To determine the future value of equal annual contributions, find the number in the "equal annual contributions" column that corresponds to your child's current age. Then multiply that number by the value of the annual investment you are considering.

  For example, if you invest $2,000 a year, beginning when your child is one, the total investment will be worth $72,900 when your child is eighteen ($2,000 times 36.45).

- To determine the future value of equal monthly contributions, find the number in the "equal monthly contributions" column that corresponds to your child's current age. Then multiply that number by the value of the monthly investment you are considering.

  For example, if you invest $200 a month, beginning when your child is two, the portfolio will be worth $77,958 when your child is eighteen ($200 times 389.79).

Calculating necessary contributions

To determine the size of a single, annual, or monthly contribution that will let you reach a given goal, simply turn the calculations around.

For example, if you want to have a portfolio worth $200,000 when your child is eighteen, go down the table to the row that corresponds to your child's current age. Then select the number in either the "single contribution," "equal annual contributions," or "equal monthly contributions" column. Divide $200,000 by the number you selected. And the answer is the investment required to reach the $200,000 goal.

For example, if your child is now three years old and you want to know the size of a single-payment investment that will reach $200,000 (at an eight percent return) when he or she is eighteen, the answer is $63,092 ($200,000 divided by 3.17).

If your child is now one and you want to make equal annual payments to reach a goal of $100,000 when he or she is eighteen, you will have to invest $2,743 a year ($100,000 divided by 36.45.)

If your child is now two years old and you want to make monthly investments to accumulate $150,000 by the time he or she is eighteen, divide $150,000 by the number corresponding to age two in the "equal monthly contributions" column. The answer is $384.82. If you invest $384.82 a month at an eight percent return, you will have $150,000 when your child is eighteen.

Extras

If you want to do more than the table on page 151 requires to reach a specific goal, you may want to consider stocks, mutual funds, precious metals, collectibles, etc.

But make sure these are "extra" investments.

Remember, the rule is: Use money you can afford to lose.

If you are very wealthy, you may be able to afford to lose it all. But being able to afford losing does not justify looking for risk.

If you want to add some riskier investments to your child's portfolio (in your child's name or in yours), it should be because they make sense. Risky investments have the "potential" to yield high returns. But you do not want to get caught up in the excitement of dealing with risk--not for your child's future.

And, of course, if you earn more or less than an eight percent return, you will have to invest less or more than what is indicated in the preceding table.

College scholarships

When your child is getting ready for college, check to see if he or she might qualify for scholarships.

Millions of dollars in scholarships go unused every year. But many of those scholarships are so narrowly defined that it is almost impossible to qualify.

In any case, scholarships come later. So you should not count on them as anything other than a possibility.

However, if you approach scholarship applications like a real job, your chances of success will improve considerably.

Prepaid college

Prepaying college tuition is a relatively new idea. It is so new that I am certain no one has yet used it. People have prepaid the future college tuition for their young children. But those children have yet to reach college age.

If such a plan seems to make sense for you and your children, check it out carefully. Is there a refund if your child decides on another school or a college in another state? What if your child decides not to go to college at all? What about entrance requirements?

Plus:

Tuition is only one part of total college costs. So do not forget about saving for the rest.

If the prepayment is for four years of tuition, do not forget that many students take six years or more to get a "four year" degree. So you may need to cover another two or more years.

Do you have to make a single payment or is there a scheduled payment plan? In either case, compare it with other alternatives. How much would you have if you invested the money in Series EE savings bonds instead? Series EE bonds should be worth at least four times your initial investment if held for 18 to 22 years. And all the earnings will be tax free if used for education. Or, what if you invested the money in zero-coupon Treasury bonds?

The point is, if you prepay tuition 18 years ahead of time, the college or state is going to invest your money. And you should think about what you can earn if you invest the money yourself.

Conclusion

I want to conclude by reminding you of the three principles of successful investing:
1) Keep it simple.
2) Relax.
3) Maintain control.

Do not get carried away with your plans or your goals. Just do what you can. When new ideas come along, compare them with the investments you are already making. But that means you had better be doing something. The ideas in this book give you something you can do, beginning today.

Many years ago, in one of his most famous poems, Robert Frost wrote the lines:
The woods are lovely, dark, and deep,
But I have promises to keep,
And miles to go before I sleep,
And miles to go before I sleep.

The world is exciting. But we only get one ride. So give your children a chance to have the best possible journey.

About the Author

Dr. Dennis Paulaha received a B.S. in Business Administration from the University of Minnesota, an M.A. in Economics from the University of Minnesota, and a Ph.D. in Economics from the University of Washington.

He was an academic economist for nine years, teaching undergraduate and graduate macroeconomic and microeconomic theory, monetary theory and policy, environmental economics, and special issues courses.

Since 1981 he has written on economic and financial issues for the public. He was Staff Economist for one of America's largest precious metals firms, and Vice President of Marketing for a brokerage company with national sales.

Dr. Paulaha's book, "The Pursuit of Happiness, An Economist's View," is used as a supplementary college text.